-£1.50

A CHOTA SAHIB

Assam and neighbouring political divisions before Independence

Assam as known to the author

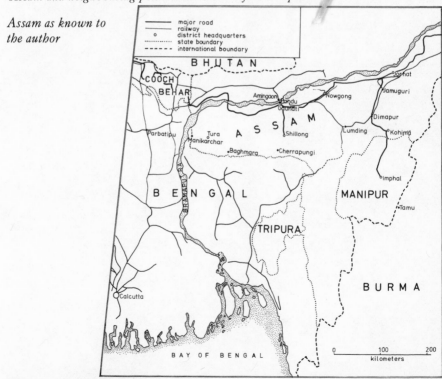

Maps prepared by Dr Katharine Rowntree

A CHOTA SAHIB

Memoirs of a Forest Officer
by
JOHN ROWNTREE

TABB HOUSE
Padstow, Cornwall

First published 1981
by Tabb House, 11 Church Street, Padstow, Cornwall.
1SBN 0 907018 04 1

Permission to reproduce the photographs by Dr Banerjee, of swamp deer, rhino, buffalo and adjutant birds, is gratefully acknowledged.

Thanks are due to Dr Rowntree for preparing the maps.

Printed in Great Britain by Quintrell & Co. Limited., Wadebridge, Cornwall.
Bound by R Booth (Bookbinders) Ltd., Carnstead, Mabe, Cornwall.

Preface

THIS ACCOUNT of the last days of the British Raj in India was written because I felt that some of my experiences were worth recording and that a description of the day-to-day life of the ordinary folk who helped to keep the wheels turning might be of interest to my family and possibly to a wider public.

The book is a miscellany of those apparently unconnected things which, nevertheless, give a society, a country or an era its character. India is full of contrasts and, although Mahatma Gandhi, the anopheles mosquito and the planters' club may appear to have had little in common, they were, in fact, closely related. If my story is sometimes serious and sometimes frivolous that, after all, is the way of life and it is of life that I have been writing.

Unfortunately, my readers cannot smell the wet earth or watch the sun set in a riot of colour across the plain; fortunately they cannot hear the ping of the mosquitos or feel the prick of their sharp probosces. Nevertheless, I hope that I have succeeded in conveying something of the atmosphere of the Indian jungle and cantonment, and in writing an honest and unbiased account of that unique and rather peculiar society, the British Raj.

Preface

Contents

List of Illustrations

Introduction

THIS IS the story of the closing years of the British Raj in India, and the chota sahibs*, the not very important people of whom I was one, who helped wind up a hundred years of British civil rule. I have called it *A Chota Sahib* because, although I became a burrasahib‡ in time, I have never been able to take myself very seriously, and it is the story of ordinary people and everyday things and is directly concerned neither with the corridors of power nor the affairs of the great. It is not a book about me nor a book about England but, as the story is told through my eyes, I can't very well keep out of it and, as the Raj was British, neither can England or the other countries of the United Kingdom. For the benefit of those with no personal knowledge of the thirties or of India it is, perhaps, relevant to describe, at this stage, the economic, social and political framework in which we worked.

It is fashionable to speak of the Raj as reactionary, which in some respects it was, but, in all fairness, what it did and what it failed to do should be viewed against the background of what Britain and other European countries were doing and failing to do at home. During the thirties the Government of India was no less concerned with the welfare of the Indian people than the British Government had been with the welfare of its own people at the turn of the century. It was believed that the poor would always be with us and *laissez faire* was still very much the economic catch phrase. It was left largely to private enterprise in both countries to raise the standard of living, materially, through industrial growth and, in India, spiritually through the missionary societies. Direct responsibility by colonial governments for growth and development and the welfare principle were new concepts which only emerged in 1945 at the end of the colonial era.

I was born in 1906, an event of no great importance. At this time an era of reform was gaining rapid momentum.

*Chota — small
‡ burra — big, important

Introduction

In India things moved more slowly. T model Fords continued to raise the dust on what passed for roads in the thirties and official residences in the *moffusil** were without piped water or sanitation.

The Indians really do have a saying *'Asti, asti bandar ko makaro',* 'softly, softly catchee monkey'. They are seldom in a hurry and, in the most reactionary indigenous society in the world it would, perhaps, have been surprising if liberal ideas had seeped through more quickly than the sewage. India still lingered nostalgically in a past which had been the present in England only some thirty years before. Perhaps the Raj deserves some praise for the fact that by 1947 she was ready for independence.

The scenery was different but the India I first knew was in many ways familiar.

The Indian *bustee,* or village, was not so very different from that of England during my youth, when the only form of public transport had been the carrier's cart. It is true that the villagers in India drew their water from wells, usually one to each village, whereas in my English village they had shared a common tap; that the cottagers in England had emptied their bowels into earth closets while the Indian peasants used the river bank, but basically there was not a great deal of difference. The Indian peasant was poor and often exploited but so, too, was the British miner. The big house in my English village was surrounded by a high wall. Its wrought iron entrance gate, through which I used to peer with the same sense of awe with which I anticipate one day, God willing, peering through the Golden Gates, was guarded by a custodian who lived in a minute and sunless lodge. In India, the Deputy Commissioner's bungalow, although no less exclusive, was less palatial, and the orderly who guarded it could at least sit in the sun.

The DC, who had assumed the mantle of the village squire, was as autocratic and as benign. His rule, like that of his English prototype, was paternal and, although he was not prepared to stand any nonsense, he had as close and usually as friendly, a relationship with his people as had the English squire with his villagers.

It was comparatively recently that the British had begun to question the status quo in their own country and it was perhaps not surprising that in India, as at home, those should be discouraged who wished to use the front door when tradition decreed that they should use the tradesman's entrance.

Superficially, to our Western eyes and noses, the India we discovered appeared to be less cultured than our own society; the gap between rich and

_____

* countryside; rural locality as opposed to chief station.

poor was wider and poverty and ignorance more extreme than anything we had imagined possible. At the same time the Indian Establishment functioned very much like our own and the rule of the District Commissioner was in line with that of the Big House in far away England. Conditioned as we were by our own upbringing, even we of the younger generation were inclined to doubt the need for administrative change, or to accept that Indians were capable of governing themselves. Being young, however, our necks and minds were still flexible and, as we came to know the Indians better, we became less sure of our ground. The older necks in the Indian establishment had grown too stiff to respond readily to the new brand of embrocation. It is, I think, greatly to the credit of these senior Europeans that, in spite of their misgivings, they co-operated so wholeheartedly in effecting the reforms, and so successfully set the stage for the transfer of power in 1947.

CHAPTER 1

Passage to India

AFTER COMING DOWN from Cambridge in 1929 I joined the Indian Forest Service. By rights I should have gone into the family business and finished up as an alderman, but I wished to be independent and had an itch to travel, which got worse after a trip to South Africa.

At the age of seventeen I had been sent to a crammer who attempted to teach me Latin and simple arithmetic, two things which an expensive boarding school had markedly failed to do. After learning three set books by heart and failing the Latin paper in the Little-go three times, I was told by a psychiatrist that I has as much chance of getting to Cambridge as I had of reaching the moon. As in 1924 this was clearly impossible, I sadly resigned myself to the inevitable. My father being a kindly and, at the time, an affluent man, sent me with a friend on a visit to the Cape, which he hoped would have the same mind-broadening effect as the Cambridge Backs and the Red Lion.

On my return I decided to have one more shot at the Little-go and, without looking at a book, set off to Cambridge to try my luck. I had so little faith in my ability as an examinee that I spent the first night in mild debauchery with an old school friend who was in his second year at the University and happened to be in residence during the long vacation. After a few drinks we decided to pay a visit to a dance hall called the Rendezvous, which was strictly out of bounds, and was raided by the proctors while we were dancing with two dumb and highly respectable girls inside. By escaping through the lavatory window and then climbing into college I managed to avoid being sent down before I had gone up. A few weeks later, much to everybody's surprise, including my own, I found myself back in residence as an undergraduate, where I began to read medicine.

When the General Strike started in 1926 my friends and I, convinced that there was a red hiding under every bed, volunteered to serve the community. Failing to get taken on as a bus driver, I found myself in the special constabulary with a tin hat on my head, an arm band and a truncheon. We were billeted in a jerry factory in Whitechapel where we slept between rows of gleaming chamber pots and once a day were drilled in the moat of the Tower of London. The so-called Red Revolution, conducted in a thoroughly

British way, was a gentlemanly affair, the only casualties being those inflicted in the boxing ring of a boys' club where we fought the strikers every night and, eventually departed the best of friends. This rather pleasant interlude was, however, marred for us by the fact that the examination for the first MB was pending, and the examiners were unpatriotic men who made no allowance in favour of those like me who had interrupted their studies in the national interest.

On failing two papers I was rusticated and departed for St Bartholomew's Hospital, having been told that I could return when I had passed the exam or if I would read almost anything but medicine, an apparently overstocked profession. After twelve uncomfortable weeks in a Knightsbridge boarding-house, I gladly returned to my Alma Mater. Being an opportunist, I switched to agriculture, chiefly because the first year syllabus was nearly identical to that of the first MB, and I hated to waste the small amount of effort I had already made. The following year I switched again, this time to Forestry, partly because I had heard it described as 'a profession fit for gentlemen', but also because I needed a job, and at that time, the foresters had more to offer than the agriculturists. I kept on the same course because I soon became fascinated with the subject, and, for the first time, became seriously interested in getting a degree. Two years later, I hesitatingly climbed the Senate House steps and scanned the list of successful candidates in the Final Examination. Starting at the last name on the list, my heart sank lower and lower as I looked in vain for my own, only to rise with unaccustomed and uncomfortable speed when I found myself at the top of the list. "You must be joking", was my father's reaction when he heard the good news. But the Godess Lachesis is a lady with a sense of humour whose favours are not always distributed deservedly.

I suppose I discovered India through reading Kipling and was to find it in many ways unchanged since his time. I chose the province of Assam on account of its off-beat character, far removed from the axe grinders of New Delhi. It was famous for its wild life, and had good shooting, fishing and cheap polo to offer — in short, the place seemed to promise just the kind of life I was looking for. There was also, I suppose, the romance of carrying the white man's burden. In those days, whatever its origins, and the history books of that day seem to have omitted some of the facts, we looked on the Empire as a civilising influence. It wasn't considered very good form to say so and I am not suggesting that the thought was uppermost in our minds when we made our choice, but it was nice to feel that one was to be usefully as well as pleasantly employed.

Having applied for jobs with both the Indian and Colonial Service, I presented myself in due course for an interview at the India Office, the Secretary of State or one of his minions having been the first to reply. Feeling full of my own importance, I was soon reduced to size by a much bemedalled ex-sergeant commissionaire, who directed me rather condescendingly along dusty corridors to a small room at the top of the building. After a few minutes' conversation, the selection board — one emaciated civilian who looked as though he had spent years pressed between sheets of blotting paper — seemed satisfied with my replies and sent me into the next room for my medical. Not, however, before he had told me that I was twenty years too late and had implied that the rats were already leaving the Imperial ship of state. He proved to be only six years out. When the Secretary of State wound up his services eighteen years later I found myself out of a job at the age of forty-one, fourteen years before I should normally have retired. This is perhaps worth mentioning because the British have been condemned for holding on to India until forced by world events to let her go. When I handed over the Provincial Forest Department in Assam to my Indian successor in 1947, he inherited a full cadre of highly-trained fellow-countrymen. This would hardly have been the case if independence had been something thought up and grudgingly conceded at the last moment.

My interview with the doctor was rather more cheerful. After telling me to swing a chair round my head and testing my heart and my blood pressure, he declared me sound in wind and limb and bid me good day. I departed, convinced that, to have got through two interviews so quickly, I must either have failed dismally, made a tremendous impression, or be the only candidate. When a letter arrived, with almost indecent haste, offering me the post of assistant conservator of forests in Assam, I decided the latter must be the case. The letter was typed on yellow paper, which I suppose was its natural hue and not the colour of age, but it smelt faintly of mould, and I accepted the offer with some foreboding. However, I decided I should have time to shoot a tiger before the ship of state finally foundered and that a free passage to India was not to be sneezed at.

With its next letter the India Office enclosed a clothes list — a far more comprehensive document than any I had received during my school days. Not only did it detail the number of handkerchiefs and pairs of underpants I should need, apparently for the next thirty years, but included a wide range of apparel suitable for any eventuality from a tiger shoot to the Viceroy's funeral. It also prescribed a white solar topee of an antiquated design, which I never wore, and a comfortable folding camp chair, which I still sit on. This was, however, to be the last occasion on which the Government of India was to show such a fatherly concern for my welfare. Once launched on my chosen career, I became another cog in the Imperial wheel, and was left to fend for myself.

Eventually the great day dawned when I boarded a P & O liner and bade a sad farewell to my parents who were standing rather forlornly on the quay. Being young, the sense of sadness soon wore off, and lured on by the smell of fresh paint, I penetrated to D deck where, in the bowels of the ship, I was to share a cabin with three other IFS recruits. During a service period of thirty years, members of the Secretary of State's Services were entitled to the cost of four return P & O first class passages. Most of us used the money to pay for more frequent but less expensive travel, but our first passage to India was invariably booked by P & O.

People who travel nonchalently by air may have missed the thrill of setting off on an ocean voyage. The great ship throbs and quivers as though she is alive and impatient to be off; tug boats hoot and launches scurry to and fro; bells ring, and the liner moves majestically out to sea like the great lady she is.

The ships of the Peninsula and Orient Line were no exception, and the Captain on his bridge was a god-like figure, almost as imposing as the Chief Purser, whose good offices were so essential to the comfort of the passengers. But the Company had the old-fashioned idea that the ship was more important than the people who had paid to sail in her and discipline both above and below decks was of the strictest. Any unfortunate who was not out of his cabin when the Captain inspected it was in serious trouble and punctuality at meals was taken for granted. Shortly before dinner the bar closed and those who were late for the meal missed whatever course or courses had already been served. Dinner jackets were worn by the men as a matter of course, and we had to fight our way into boiled shirts even when the ship was sailing with a following wind through the Red Sea. The boat deck was out of bounds after dark and the different classes were rigorously segregated on their respective decks.

Apart from the new recruits who had no choice in the matter, those who had chosen to travel in this way were for the most part burrasahibs — soldiers who commanded regiments and battalions, civil servants who held senior posts in the secretariat, the occasional provincial governor, and, of course, their ladies, the burramems. There were also a few top business men who were there on sufferance and were referred to as boxwallahs, a somewhat derogatory term more properly applicable to itinerant tradesmen. On board our ship there were two brothers, one an army colonel and the other the manager of a tea estate. The colonel's lady, jealous of her station, never, as far as I know, spoke to her less exalted sister-in-law. There was also some manoeuvering for position between the civilian members of the civil services and the soldiers. In India there was, and still may be, as far as I know, a document known as 'the table of precedence', an invaluable work of reference for memsahibs, decreeing who should sit next to whom at dinner parties. Although the document equates both military and civilian ranks, it has never officially been decided whether the sun shines out of the military or civilian navel. As can be imagined it was a happy company who coldly eyed those chosen to sit at the captain's table.

There was a rather frightening woman at our table, who claimed to be descended from Henry VIII, and behaved as though she was. If she did not gnaw bones and throw them onto the floor, it was only because there were no dogs on board, and the ship's cats, being P & O cats, did not appear at meal times. She was however as domineering and grasping as the father of the first Elizabeth. At the beginning of dinner she would select the choicest fruits from the dish which adorned the centre of the table and place them firmly in front of her soup plate, to be eaten later, while we lesser mortals offered one another the left-overs. Also on board were a number of young ladies reputed to be just as acquisitive. These were the daughters of the burramems. There were no teenagers in those days, just 'girls' and 'gels', and if you weren't a young lady you were a young woman. The gels had for the most part just left school and were reputedly all looking for husbands, a notoriously easy task in India. They were known as the 'fishing fleet' and were cultivated or avoided, according to the disposition of the young gentlemen. As few of us had been devoid of female company in the immediate past, they were mostly avoided. In any case, I managed to complete the voyage with a free heart, in spite of or, perhaps, because of, their mums.

The time at sea passed pleasantly if uneventfully. There was the usual ship's bore who insisted on over-organising deck sports, which would otherwise have been an enjoyable means of passing the time. There was the fancy dress ball, a slightly less restrained function than most, and a visit to a rather seamy-sided Marseilles. We were offered dirty postcards at Port Said, saw a mirage and some camels in the Canal zone and suffered from prickly heat in the Red Sea. We watched the dolphins and the flying fish, wondered how anyone could live from choice on that great slag heap known as Aden, and finally berthed in the docks at Bombay.

Seen from the sea, with its white houses and fringe of palm trees, Bombay was a beautiful place. The streets were reasonably clean and there was usually a sea breeze. On closer inspection, it was very like any other Indian city. The docks were a mad house of semi-naked coolies, all yelling at the top of their voices, and we descended into what appeared to be a riot but was, in fact, just a normal working day. As I left the ship, I couldn't help feeling there was something to be said for its iron discipline.

It was nice to feel firm ground under one's feet after three weeks at sea and exciting to be setting out in an unknown land, but, at the same time, my future appeared to be disconcertingly uncertain. On our arrival at Bombay, my three travelling companions had each received written instructions on how to proceed to their destinations. I received no instructions at all. Later I was to learn that, after issuing me with a clothes list, the Secretary of State had forgotten all about me and the Government of Assam had yet to discover that it was about to welcome a new recruit. This was not altogether surprising because, as it turned out, I should not have been there at all. At this time Indianisation of the Services was proceeding rapidly and it was Assam's turn to get an Indian recruit in the Forest Service. The last man to have joined was however, an Irishman called Bor, and Bor, with a different spelling, is a common Indian name. The India Office was convinced that Bor was an Indian and that the next appointment should be European. Quite innocently I had done some Indian lad out of a job.

I had also been lucky in another way. Assam had been suffering from that common complaint, financial stringency, and prior to my appointment there had been no recruitment to the IFS in that province for some years. At a later date, the All-India Services were provincialised and members serving in one province were no longer eligible for promotion to senior posts in another. As a result, with no promotion block, I found myself at the top long before I should normally have expected to get there. Again, unknown to me, my Karma was in good hands, and the joke was that my colleages were unable to understand why I had chosen Assam, which they wrongly considered the most backward province in India.

But to return to Bombay. Eventually I found my way to the railway station and asked the booking clerk for a ticket to Shillong, the seat of the Assam Government. "To what part will you be wanting ticket?" inquired the babu*, emphasising his query with an explosive belch. This seemed to me rather an odd question because I imagined Shillong to be quite a small place, unlikely to have more than one railway station. Fortunately, I discovered in the nick of time that we were at cross purposes — the clerk thought I had said Ceylon, which is quite a large island, and was about to send me to the southern tip of India instead of its north east frontier. Considerable research in a number of timetables disclosed the fact that Shillong had no railway station at all and

* a clerk

was, indeed, some sixty miles from a rail head. Armed with a ticket for a place called Amingaon, the next problem was to transport a large and varied assortment of luggage to the waiting train. Fortunately a mob of eager coolies emerged from the wings and twelve of the more dynamic seized a piece of baggage each and bore it away on his head in what proved to be the right direction.

Seated at last in a comfortable first class compartment, I next had to decide how much to tip this army of baggage carriers. When I finally presented each with a rupee, then worth one shilling and sixpence, pandemonium broke loose. The correct rate was about four pence. The coolies obviously considered that anyone green enough to pay them such largesse was fool enough to part with more. Just as a riot appeared inevitable, the train gathered itself together and drew out of the station.

I found myself in sole occupation of a commodious compartment with a padded seat running along each of its outside walls, two bunks folded back above, an arm-chair and table and two electric fans. The compartment also had its own bathroom and lavatory complete with shower. Alone in my glory I gazed out of the windows at a strange land of low, parched, red hills, through a haze of dust, which soon began to penetrate the cracks in the doors and windows and which, every so often, when the train stopped at some station, was spread around by a sweeper. This sweeper was not, of course, just anyone with a broom, but a member of the untouchable sweeper caste, the lowest form of human being.

As the sweeper could not remove the dust from my body, I decided to have a cooling and cleansing shower. Stripping, I entered the bathroom, stood under the shower, pulled the chain and, crying out in agony, shot back naked into the compartment — the water tank, situated on the roof and heated by the sun, was full of boiling water. Unable to open the windows because of the dust, or to bathe because the water was red hot, first class travel began to lose some of its promised charm.

There was no corridor in the train and no restaurant car. Instead, while the engine let off steam impatiently outside, we ate at station restaurants along the route, gulping down our cold soup, tough old boiling fowls and caramel custard, fearful that we should be left stranded with the beggars on the platform. Eventually, the engine would start to whistle impatiently, we would hastily pay the bill and hurry back to the train, which would remain motionless for another thirty minutes before the whistling stopped and it moved off.

During this half hour a crowd of beggars would collect outside the compartment to display their deformities, their stumps, sores and sightless eyes and to demand baksheesh in a penetrating whine — the most nerve-racking sound on earth. If they got nothing, their whine continued; if they got what they wanted, it continued just the same. When our nerves were frayed beyond endurance, the beggars would eventually depart under a shower of abuse, leaving their victims feeling guilty, impotent and completely exhausted.

The beggars of India have remained an apparently insoluble problem. They existed in their millions under the British Raj and, I understand, they still exist in their millions today. I am told there are no beggars in Communist China. If so, Communism seems to have succeeded in this one respect where Democracy has failed. Many Indians have been hungry at one time or another, and have had to beg. There are also the holy men, to whom alms are given as an act of grace. However, the vast army of professional beggars, the most wretched dregs of humanity, are a disgrace to any country, and should not be tolerated. The appalling fact is that there seems to be nothing one can do as an individual. Like doctors who have to treat distressing cases, one just gets used to them. As the Turkish proverb puts it: 'He who weeps for the world won't have any eyes left.'

Indian railway stations are bizarre places. At night we picked our way through the dim light over what appeared to be a sea of corpses, but which were, in reality, sleepers, tightly wrapped like cocoons in frayed blankets, waiting for their trains. The air was filled with the beggars' whining and the more cheerful signature tune of the tea and betel nut vendors — *'guram char, pan,* cigarettes.' A red-turbanned policeman watched from the shadows. Suddenly, as if roused by some railway Gabriel, the sleepers would rise as one man and make for the bare and uncomfortable third-class coaches of a newly-arrived train.

Had I realised it, this enforced and rather lonely period of isolation in a first class compartment was no bad introduction to the India of the Raj. The microcosmic, but not always so comfortable, life of the sahibs in their small Anglo-Indian world was one from which we sometimes ventured but, inhibited by social convention, were seldom able to make any real contact with the people of the country.

It took our train nearly three days to reach Calcutta and, as we travelled further east, the countryside grew greener, damper and slightly less dusty. Buffaloes replaced oxen in the plough teams, rice took the place of wheat in the fields, and instead of being baked in a hot oven, we sweated it out in a hothouse atmosphere. The rice being harvested and the sheaves carried home, hung on long poles borne on the shoulders of semi-naked, quick stepping villagers; the golden paddy fields stretched across the flat plain as far as the eye could reach. Clusters of palms marked the sites of villages — groups of thatched mud huts with the occasional tin-roofed house of some more opulent villager. Small children naked except for a string round their tummies, rode fearlessly on the backs of fierce looking buffaloes; bullock carts creaked along dusty lanes and a solitary car would disappear along a dirt track in a cloud of dust. As night fell, the sky, for a few minutes, was splashed with glorious colour and white paddy birds flew to their roosts against a backcloth of golds and flaming reds which would have delighted Turner or Monet. The air was full of the most alluring of all scents, the smell of damp earth.

At Calcutta I developed a fever and took to my bed at the Great Eastern Hotel. Foolishly, I had bought a Family Doctor, a book from which I gathered that families in India were subject to an alarming number of diseases. I could not be certain whether I was suffering from cholera, beri beri, plague or blackwater fever, but felt as though I had the lot. The Indian doctor, who came to my assistance, could find nothing specifically the matter with me and, perhaps exorcised by his diagnosis, the fever left me as rapidly as it had appeared.

Unfortunately, I then discovered that, not only the fever, but most of my money, was spent. Believing, however, that it would not be difficult for a member of one of the Secretary of State's Services to recoup his finances, I set forth confidently in search of the Secretariat, the seat of the Bengal Government. In this I was proved to be wrong. I had not realised that, while I was tossing on my sick bed, something called the *Durga Puja* had begun — an annual Hindu festival, during which the Government of India goes into retreat and takes a three week's holiday. When I arrived at the Secretariat, the doors were shut and barred and not a soul was in sight.

Fortunately, money was not an important means of exchange within the hotel where, until the final day of reckoning, a signature on a chit caused the iced drinks to flow freely. But, once having left its doors, I found myself in a hard, unsympathetic world. Chevrolet taxis sped by driven by bearded Sikhs, whom I could not afford to employ. Even the strings of overworked tram cars were beyond my slender means. I tramped for miles along dusty streets, visited bazaars full of choice wares I could not buy and was barred from enjoying the air-conditioned comfort of the 'bioscope'.

Calcutta was, I had been told, fun. A good place for a European to be stationed, with lots to do, delightful clubs and a good golf course. To the poor it had less to offer and the homeless slept on its pavements and urinated in its gutters. The city sprawled over the Hooghly Delta like a disease — a dirty, overcrowded town of slums and belching factory chimneys. Scattered among the newer buildings were the *bustees* — once villages, whose huts somehow survived in the shadow of the tenements — where the villagers drew water from ancient wells, and drainage systems had yet to be devised. At night the pariah dogs scavenged for titbits among the garbage, and the beggars rested from their labours. It was not a town to be proud of.

I found my way to the Calcutta Zoo which was cheap but depressing — a beautiful park where polar bears panted and sweated (if a bear can sweat) under a hot sun; tigers endlessly patrolled their small cages and eagles looked longingly at the sky. Finding this zoo distasteful, I returned disheartened through shady streets where the burrasahibs lived in their comfortable air-conditioned bungalows. Now, having lived myself in the wilderness, I hate all zoos. Passions run high over hunted foxes, animals whose numbers, after all, have to be controlled. Few people ever spare a thought for those unfortunate animals that have lost both freedom and dignity by being condemned to live unhappy and unnatural lives in cages.

Every so often, I would return to the Secretariat in the faint hope that I might find somebody at work and, after a week, I did. He was a kindly Bengali, a middle-grade civil servant who seemed to have taken on his shoulders the responsibilities of an entire nation. He listened to my tale of woe, regretted that he could not give me an official 'sub' until the office reopened, but made me a small personal loan. That night I boarded the train for Assam.

The train passed through more paddy fields and more identical *bustees* and, as night fell, under the same blood red sky. In the middle of the night the train departed for Srinagar, leaving the Assam passengers marooned on the platform at Parbatipur Junction. Here, we eventually transferred ourselves and our luggage to the Assam-Bengal Railway, a single line affair of Victorian vintage but un-Victorian unsteadiness, and of an independent character seldom found today. Its trains have been known to halt while memsahibs picked flowers and their menfolk shot snipe and has, to my own knowledge, been stopped by wild elephants. My bunk was only just long enough for my six feet and, being situated immediately above a bogie, as my compartment appeared to have square wheels, I did not get much sleep. However, in spite of the rock-and-roll effect, it was a friendly sort of railway, which I have always remembered with affection.

In the early hours of a surprisingly cold and misty morning, we reached Amingaon on the north bank of the River Brahmaputra. Coolies shivered, their heads shrouded in blankets, and a European lad, on his way to take up an appointment as an assistant on a tea garden, dissolved into tears. Our spirits rose as the air was filled with the smell of frying bacon and strong coffee and we were soon breakfasting in a spotlessly clean ferry steamer — a real showboat of a steamer, complete with paddles and, one suspected, card sharpers asleep in the cabins. We were ferried across a mile of water to Pandu on the south bank. Here the passengers for Shillong climbed into the cars of the Shillong Motor Company and, as the sun rose, began the last lap of their journey.

CHAPTER 2

Strange New World

THE ROAD to Shillong climbs 4,000 feet in sixty miles and is a succession of hair-rising hairpin bends which have often been the undoing of queasy stomachs. At that time, it was a single track with a series of gates to control the traffic, and a passing point for those going up and down at Nongpo. An excellent system, as long as one arrived on time.

The road starts its climb through sal forest which, if it were not for the bamboos, has much the same character as an English oak wood. Then the broadleaf trees begin to give way to pines and finally to bare, grass-covered slopes and plateaux, the hills being cut by deep gorges. Shillong is the capital of the Khasi and Jaintia Hills, in those days native states. Like all the hill tribes in Assam, the Khasis practice *juming,* or shifting cultivation, a system which worked well enough when wars and disease kept the population in check. Now it has grown to such an extent that, over much of the hills, disforestation is complete and erosion has set in. But the Khasis still depended on ashes to fertilise their crops and, if there were no trees left to fell, brought brushwood from a distance to burn on their cultivated land. *Juming* is one of the most serious problems in the hills of India and one which we, in our time, failed to solve, despite many attempts to do so. In the reserved forests, villagers were allowed to *jum* in unproductive areas, on the condition that they planted the land with trees when they moved on, a practice known as *taungya,* but this hardly touched the fringe of the problem. In a few places, they were persuaded to adopt a system of permanent terraced cultivation, but the hill men are a conservative lot, reluctant to change their ways, and the politicians took a lot of persuading that they should do so.

We drove through the forest to an accompaniment of cicadas, which made such a persistent din that we only really noticed it when they grew tired and stopped their chirruping. Then we were in the open country above with Shillong nestling in a hollow below us. With its neat white houses among the pine trees it might have been one of the more select holiday resorts on the west coast of Scotland — the Gurkha troops stationed there even had their pipe band and were proficient pipers.

In Shillong I hired a taxi and, for want of a better address, told the driver to take me to the Secretariat. We set off past an ornamental lake surrounded by pine trees, the Club with its red tennis courts, and through a pair of massive wrought iron gates where a Gurkha guard sprang smartly to attention and presented arms. The car sped up a long drive flanked by trees and banked with flower beds, and halted in front of an imposing building surrounded by trim lawns. A *chaprasi* in a scarlet tunic salaamed and disappeared, to return with an elegantly dressed young man who eyed me rather coldly and asked what he could do for me.

The young man proved to be the Governor's ADC and, unwashed and unshaven and wearing a filthy pair of Khaki shorts and sweat stained shirt, I stood under the Union Jack in front of Government House, trying to give a rational explanation of why I was there. As the secretaries were apparently still playing golf or tennis, it was no use making a fresh attempt to reach the Secretariat. Instead, I was directed to the Pinewood Hotel where I was given a little chalet bungalow to myself and was able to make myself presentable.

At the hotel I fell in with a Scot who was a tea planter but not, I was to discover, noticeably a tea drinker. We went together that evening to the club where he downed a surprising number of whisky pegs and insisted that I did likewise. At least, that was his intention but, fortunately, he didn't seem to notice whether I actually did any drinking. As he became increasingly argumentative, and the other drinkers in the bar were eyeing us with some hostility, I thought it best to accept the drinks without demur and had soon acquired quite a collection. I began to wonder what kind of an impression I should make on my chief if our first meeting were to take place in the company of my new friend.

The meeting eventually took place in the Club lavatory. "I believe you're Rowntree," said the great man, buttoning up his flies, and adding that he would have been delighted to put me up but was sure I was more comfortable where I was. He then asked me about my interests and I ventured "birds", but he was speaking, not of hobbies, but of professional interests, and it was decided that I should join the provincial silviculturist at a place called Jorhat. Silviculture is the science or art of growing trees and, the silviculturist was called Paddlebum because his real name was Rowbothom. Having given me this information, the great man departed and shortly afterwards left Assam for good to enjoy what was, no doubt, a well earned retirement. I piloted home a very drunk Scotsman and the next day collected some money and drove back down the hill to board a train for Jorhat and Upper Assam.

The geography of Assam is not easy to understand, but I will do my best to describe it. Before partition, the province was roughly the size of England and Wales, shaped like a cloven hoof, rimmed by jungle-clad mountains and with the pastern joint of the hoof pointing towards China. To the north the Himalayas separate Assam from Tibet and are crowned by four peaks: Gari Chen, Kangdu, Chumo and Nyegi Kainsang — all over 22,000 feet high and covered with deliciously cool white, sometimes blue or pink, icing. To the east lies China, on the other side of the Namkin Mountains, and to the south, beyond the Patkoi Range, the Naga and Lushai Hills and the State of Manipur, is Burma. At the junction of the pastern joint and the hoof a central dividing range, a westerly offshoot from the Naga Hills, forms the frog. This comprises the North Cachar, Jaintia, Khasi and Garro hills which separates the Assam, or Brahmaputra Valley, to the north from the Surma Valley to the south. Halfway up the pastern joint another offshoot, the Mikir Hills, is joined by a narrow neck to the Naga Hills and runs north as far as the Brahmaputra which flows down the centre of the valley.

The Brahmaputra rises in Tibet, where it is known as the Tsangpo, flows east for about 300 miles, cuts through the Himalayas into upper Assam, at Sadiya, and then flows west for another 250 miles or so through the Assam Valley before turning south and joining the Ganges in what is now Bangladesh.

The population of Assam — a medley of Indo-Aryan and Tibeto-Burman races — is, if anything, even more complicated than the geography. The Ahoms of upper Assam who have given their name to the state, — slant-eyed, flat-faced migrants from China, — crossed into Burma and, sometime during the 13th century, continued their migration northwards. Crossing the Naga Hills they drove the Cacharis, a Bodo people, from their capital, with its great phallic megaliths, at Dimapur, and established themselves in upper Assam. The Cacharis retreated into the North Cachar Hills and, later, into what was to become the district of Cachar in the Surma Valley. In 1515 there was a Cooch dynasty in lower Assam and in 1527 a Muslim invasion. Hinduism became the predominant religion during the 18th century.

The British first arrived in 1816, when they were asked by the Ahoms to drive out the Burmese who had invaded their country. The Burmese withdrew and, on this occasion, the British decided to stay, and imposed their direct rule in Assam in 1826.

Since then, land-hungry immigrants, chiefly Muslims from Bengal, have emigrated to Assam and have made their homes there. Assam, if not a land of milk and honey, is flowing with water and endowed with fertile soil. It must be the easiest place in India from which to win a living. The Assamese are, as a result, an easy going people, (some would say lazy; others sensible), who like an easy life and object to doing any work other than the minimum required to grow their crops. Tea estates have to recruit labour from the less fertile parts of India. Timber merchants rely on Nepalis to convert the trees, and imported coolies are almost invariably employed in public works. Many of these immigrant labourers have acquired land of their own and become Assamese; the merchants are Marwaris, the shoemakers are, or were, Chinese; the motor mechanics, Sikhs, and the graziers, Nepalis.

Then there are the hill tribes, some slowly emerging from the early Iron Age, some of whom prefer to go about naked, or wearing artificial tails. Others like collecting peoples' heads as a hobby and some tribesmen are dab hands with a poisoned dart. Most of these primitives appear to be remnants of the various Mongol tribes from central Asia which were left behind during their southern migrations — the Nagas are thought to have cultural links with Indonesia and Melanesia. Today, some sixty distinct languages are spoken in Assam, but, fortunately, modern Assamese, which is something like Bengali, has become the common language and is usually understood by somebody, even in the more remote villages.

Few of these facts were known to me as I set off on my travels once more from Gauhati, the nearest railway station to Shillong, on a clear, scintillating morning at the beginning of the cold weather. The train puffed its way across paddy fields carpeted with golden rice stubble and then, squeezing between the Mikir and Naga Hills, the single-track tunnelled through fifty miles of evergreen and seemingly endless forest, which pressed threateningly towards the track on either side. Eventually we emerged once more into the open and, finally, after changing onto a branch line, I arrived at my destination.

Jorhat turned out to be a sprawling, untidy place on the dead flat alluvial plain of the Brahmaputra valley, surrounded by tea gardens, which is what the Assam tea plantations are called, and which are not necessarily places where one drinks tea. At the centre of the town was the *maidan,* a large open piece of grass surrounded by gold mohur trees, with flowers only a little less glamorous than their name.

For the time being, I was to live in solitary state in the circuit house, which was one of the official bungalows surrounding the *maidan,* and the temporary residence of judges on circuit, other senior officials on their tours of inspection, and homeless odds and sods like me. It was a soulless place which, like most Assam bungalows, had whitewashed reed and plaster walls (cement plaster had only recently replaced cowdung in most of them) and a red tin roof. It was raised on stilts. This custom is said to have stemmed from the old belief that malaria was induced by mist, and the idea was to raise the living quarters above the danger level. In these more enlightened times, the raised floors of the bungalows provided useful car porches, but the numerous posts from which the walls were suspended — a precaution against earthquakes — sometimes caused problems. Once, I returned late from the club and, as usual, drove the car under my bungalow, parking it in what appeared to be an open space. The next morning, posts, which had apparently grown in the night, hemmed it in on all sides. It took me half an hour's skilful manoeuvering to get the car out — how it got in, remains a mystery. The light lath and plaster walls were another anti-earthquake device and little harm was done if the plaster was shaken off. However, they tended to get a bit soft in wet weather. In one of my bungalows, the dining-room was at ground level, and below the level of the suspended floor, which also provided shelter for a number of itinerant cows. One of these creatures poked its head through the wall one morning at breakfast time. I thought she looked quite decorative over the sideboard, but my newly-wedded wife got quite a shock.

The Jorhat circuit house had large bare rooms and a spacious veranda. The only decor was provided by friendly little green lizards that ran up and down or clung motionless stuck to the walls by means of suckers on their feet. The furnishing consisted of a few massive pieces, which had been made with a remarkable lack of taste during the reign of the Queen Empress. Each monstrosity bore a large PWD, standing for Public Works Department, branded on its flank. The woodwork was treated with earth oil which came off on our clothes if we leaned against it. Bedding, cutlery, cooking pots and food to cook had to be provided by each occupant, and the cooking itself was done outside in a smoky communal cookhouse that did not bear too close an inspection. Milk and water had to be boiled before they were safe to drink. The bath water was collected from a communal tap on the road outside, and then heated in a kerosene tin before being poured into a tin tub. Paddle, the silviculturist, lived next door in a rose-covered bungalow, which was later to become my home, and on the other side was the *dak* * bungalow for non-official travellers, which had a similar format to the circuit house but boasted rather more bugs.

My first priority was to engage a cook-bearer, a small, bearded Muslim called Abdul who wore blacker than black baggy 'white' trousers, a grimy pullover and a fez and who produced his *hisab,* or bill, daily for my inspection. As was to be expected he took his cut on all bazaar purchases, but I didn't realise, until I married, that a dozen eggs a day was anything out of the ordinary for a solitary bachelor.

My first task, I discovered, was a round of calls. Instead of waiting to be called on, as was the custom in England, the newcomers were expected to do the calling. In return, they either received an invitation at a later date, or else

*Government bungalow for the use of travelling officials.

were ignored. Naturally, I had to call at all the official bungalows. The Deputy Commissioner, Superintendent of Police, District Engineer and Inspector of Schools, as well, of course, as the Divisional Forest Officer, were the most important. Fortunately for me, Jorhat possessed no Commissioner or resident Judge, which would have added two more to the list. Then there was the superintendent of the local tea company, the tea garden managers and the American Baptist missionaries. There were no Indians on my calling list, except for two of the officials.

Having bought a bicycle, I changed into a spotless white suit and started on my round. Arriving at the first bungalow on my list for the day, I would button up my sweat-soaked shirt, reluctantly fasten my tie and pull on my coat before entering the compound. There were no bells and I found that callers were expected to stand on the veranda steps and call "*quoi hai*" ("Is anyone there"?) at the top of their voices — something of an ordeal to a rather self-conscious young man. Eventually a servant would appear and bear off one's card. With luck, nobody would be at home. With rather less luck, the occupier of the bungalow would turn out to be a bachelor, and, at the very worst, the lady of the house would be at home and offer one tea. A friend of mine was once being entertained in this way by a very grand lady, after having spent some weeks in the jungle. He had been in the habit of taking tea out-of-doors in front of his tent, and throwing the dregs from his cup over his shoulder into the undergrowth. Unfortunately, he absent-mindedly repeated this performance in his hostess's immaculate drawing-room.

One of the Indians was a bachelor. The other was married but his wife was in purdah, and all I saw of these two bungalows were the verandas.

At last, having left the required number of cards, I was free to do some work, but Paddle seemed to find this rather a problem. He eventually presented me with a flora of Indian trees, a weighty tome by a gentleman called Brandis, and told me to copy out the descriptions of the commoner Assam species. Fortunately, he never asked to see my handiwork for, realising that the information was to be had in the office library whenever it was needed, I did not take this exercise very seriously.

After a few days, Paddle, having concluded that I would never make a silviculturist or, perhaps, that I was a blot on the landscape, decided that I should go into the jungle and build a road. With considerable relief, I gathered up my bedding holdall, a large box full of stores, a tent, a couple of suitcases, some camp furniture, my bicycle, a basketful of live chickens and Abdul. Then I entrained once more, this time for only a short railway journey.

At Jamaguri, more of a halt than a station, two large elephants were waiting for us. On our arrival, they prostrated themselves and salaamed with upraised trunks, remaining in this position while my kit was strung, like presents on a Christmas tree, on top of one of them, and I had clambered onto the back of the other. Howdahs are only used by the truly great, at least in Assam, and I sat precariously perched on a *gadi,* a kind of mattress, while the mahout sat in front on the animal's neck and directed it with his bare toes. The elephants lurched to their feet and I clutched my mahout desperately round his neck. Once my elephant was in a horizontal position I felt relatively safe, but riding on a pad is rather like riding on top of a car on a bumpy road and is not to be recommended if one can walk on one's own two feet. Fortunately we had only a mile to go along a dirt track which wound through a forest of blue flowering *Eupotorium* which, like the water hyacinth, has somehow spread to Assam from across the sea and taken firm root.

I was to spend the night at the Jamaguri forest rest house, a rather pleasant two-roomed building with a thatched roof and a large, shady veranda. At least, it seemed pleasant enough as I crept under the mosquito net and settled down to a well-earned rest, but in the middle of the night I had a disturbing dream, in which one of the elephants had gone berserk and was doing its best to demolish the bungalow. I awoke with a start to discover that the building was indeed rocking in an alarming way, leapt out of bed and fell flat on my face. On all fours I crawled into the open to find that this was no dream but that the elephants were not to blame. It was just an earthquake, one of Assam's little jokes. Compared to some it was not much of a 'quake, but first impressions are always interesting. I have known earthquakes when steam rose through fissures in the ground and, on one occasion, every inch of plaster was shaken off the walls, yet only one china ornament was broken while brick buildings collapsed like card houses. Assam's earthquakes have diverted rivers and flooded square miles of land, but this one did little damage, and being young, I was soon asleep again.

Our journey the next day was fifteen miles into the forest at the foot of the Naga Hills and, wisely, I rode my bicycle instead of the elephant. The dirt road, though impossible during the rains, was now hard and formed a reasonable cycle track, as long as one avoided the major bumps. My guide was Bonomali Das, the local forester. He was a charming but rather simple fellow who wore an old-fashioned and very broad-brimmed hard topee on his head. In his youth, an elephant apple, a large and extremely hard fruit about the size of a coconut and almost of the same consistency, had fallen on his head, which may have accounted for both his present choice of hat and, to some extent, for his simplicity. Although his I Q was rather low, he proved to be a tower of strength.

Somewhat naturally, I expected to find a tiger sitting behind every bush but all we saw, as we pedalled through the forest, were schools of noisy gibbons, called hoolocks by the Assamese after their call; some brightly-coloured birds and, once, a barking deer that leapt across the track. It took me a long time to accept the fact that the Assam jungle was a less dangerous place to negotiate than Piccadilly Circus, and to discard my gun in favour of an umbrella. A brolly may seem an odd thing to have carried, but it is good protection from the sun and keeps one dry during the rains when the humidity is at 90 per cent, and a mackintosh would be unacceptable. It can also, at times, be used effectively as a weapon. A colleague, when confronted by an angry bear on one occasion, opened his umbrella in its face and left bruin struggling with this strange animal while he beat a hasty retreat. But, except for bears who can't see very well, and are suspicious of strangers as a result, most wild animals do their best to get out of one's way. They seldom attack unless wounded, cornered, or believe their young to be in danger. The exceptions are the occasional man-eating tigers and leopards, and rogue elephants, but in their case one is usually forewarned and forearmed.

Our camp was on the high bank of the Horupani River, whose clear waters cascaded from the Naga Hills in a series of deep pools and rapids. In the pools, mahseer, the giant carp of India, which weigh up to 60 lb, could be taken on a spoon, if one were both lucky and clever enough. The pools were also wonderful places in which to bathe, if one didn't mind sharing them with the crocodiles. Fortunately, the Assamese crocs are gorials, the long-nosed, fish-eating variety, and do not attack man, but one always had the uncomfortable feeling that perhaps they might make an occasional exception.

The job in hand was to improve the existing track and turn it into an extraction road but, having served only a short apprenticeship in surveying, and forgotten most of what I had learnt, I wondered what sort of a figure I should cut. I need not have worried because the elephants had done the surveying for us — that is, the wild elephants. Our own were used as bulldozers to uproot small trees and pick them out of the debris, like experienced spillikin players.

The Assam forests are honeycombed with *dandies,* that is, elephant tracks, beaten hard by the feet of generations of elephants. Some cross the hills into Burma, while others extend along the foot of the Himalayas as far as what were, in our time, the United Provinces. Elephants have an eye, or nose, which is far more effective than a theodolite in wooded country, and an unerring instinct for choosing the most suitable alignment. All one had to do to make a road, was to widen an existing *dandi,* altering the alignment slightly where the elephants had been content to walk through a swamp instead of going round it.

The smaller jungle was cleared by Naga coolies, with their beautifully-balanced jungle knife, the *dao*, which they also sometimes use to cut off their own fingers, and other people's heads. They cut off their fingers if bitten by a snake, before the venom has a chance to spread; they cut off heads because they are head-hunters. The winning of a head is the mark of manhood, and used to be a necessary preliminary to marriage, while the severed head is itself valued because it is the repository of the victim's soul, and this becomes the slave of whoever owns the head. A baby's head is one of the most coveted, because to win such a trophy usually means penetrating an enemy village.

Head-hunting was uncommon by the time I arrived in Assam, but old men still wore brass heads, each representing a human kill, and tattoo marks told the same tale. The younger men were content to wear necklaces of boar's tusks or tiger's teeth to prove their manhood. All this was unknown to me, as my Nagas sat round the camp fire at night and roared with laughter as they listened to 'Horsey, Keep Your Tail Up' and other recent hits on my gramophone. Otherwise, I might have found these musical evenings less enjoyable.

The Naga is a short, thickset, golden-skinned hill man, with slanting eyes and a bob of black hair. In his own village, he wears very little, and sometimes goes naked. He cuts his hair by placing a piece of wood between it and his head and trimming his locks against the chopping board with his *dao*. He is usually cheerful and a better friend than an enemy. The Nagas used to delight in raiding the plains and they still refer to the plainsmen disdainfully as *Kala Admi* or blackmen. Nowadays, however, they earn money in the low country during the cold weather, clearing land of jungle, to buy salt and various luxuries which they take home to the hills. While working, the Nagas chant in unison — a series of not very musical but impressive grunts, and when they are not working they drink rice beer, which they brew in quantity. They are also hunters and fishermen, and, like all the hill tribes, practice shifting cultivation, or *juming*. The jungle is cleared, burnt, cultivated and finally abandoned after growing its crop. As the population is always on the move, they are constantly building new villages, and, as these are named after headmen who are constantly dying, maps soon get out of date and are not a great deal of use.

In his bachelor days, the Naga youth is a promiscuous lover, but once married becomes a faithful husband. Otherwise he and his lady-friend are apt to die, each painfully secured at the growing tip of a bamboo which slowly penetrates their genital organs, or such, at one time, was the punishment.

The Naga Hills were first explored in 1830, and were partly administered in 1880. Eighty-two years later, in 1962, the Nagas forced the Indian Government to recognise Nagaland as an independent state within the Indian federation. The Nagas are slowly coming to terms with the 20th century, and now nearly thirty per cent are literate. The year 1970 was the first in which a PhD was awarded to a Naga by an Indian university and, at the time of writing, records the last known case of head hunting.

When work was over for the day, I would try and bag something for the pot. Occasionally, I would stalk and shoot one of the game little jungle fowl, which seldom get off the ground in thick jungle, or one of the still more secretive, long-tailed peacock pheasants, which like to skulk in the undergrowth. There were also the fat, piguma pigeons with their booming call, and the little green pigeons which shot through the air at incredible speed. Evergreen forest is not, however, the best place for game, which prefers open country. Nor was game easy to detect in the thick undergrowth, mixed with bamboos and canes, festooned with wreathing lianes, some as thick as a man's body, and hidden in deep shade. Finding one's way was even more difficult, because the ground was dead flat and devoid of landmarks, while one piece of forest looked very like the next. To add to one's difficulties, progress was constantly being interrupted by the presence of swamps and cane brakes, which had to be circumvented, and which made it difficult to preserve any sense of direction. If one got lost the only thing to do was to try to find a stream, and follow it to the river. Somehow, I always got back, but usually without anything for the pot.

The Assam cold weather is delightful — as the morning mist clears, successive layers of clothing are peeled off until, finally, the sun is shining in a clear sky and one is down to one's shirt. In the evening it is cold enough to enjoy a fire. At night, the jungle comes to life — an elephant trumpets in the distance, a tiger coughs menacingly, and man, but a puny creature, quickly throws another log on the fire.

I returned to Jorhat for Christmas, a rather lonely one, where, being a new boy, I felt rather out of it. The sahibs made merry at the planters' club, played golf, tennis and polo, drank whisky pegs, lost or won money at bridge and poker and, in a few cases, went to church. The young men danced to a gramophone in what was familiarly called the snake pit, made love, or swapped yarns at the bar. One of them insisted on walking into the night through an upstairs window, but, being drunk, came to no harm.

After Christmas, I was back at Jamaguri, this time in search of a man-eating tiger. Man-eaters are, fortunately, not common — this was the only one I had anything to do with during my eighteen years in the Assam jungle

— but they are difficult customers to deal with. The normal way to shoot a tiger in thickly-wooded country is to sit over a kill. In more open country, they can be driven out of cover by elephants or men. The Garos surround them with nets, gradually reducing the circumference until the tiger is within range of their spears. The Nagas do the same thing without a net, encircling the tiger with a human wall of spearmen which gradually closes in on the hunted animal. But man-eaters are suspicious by nature, although they have lost their initial fear of man, and seem to be more cautious than the normal tiger. They are usually old animals that can no longer hunt four-legged prey successfully, or younger ones that have been wounded. Once they have tasted human flesh, they appear to acquire a taste for it. This particular man-eater had killed several sawyers who were working in the forest, and work was at a standstill, but nobody had been able to get a shot at him.

He appeared to have a good appetite, because he finished off his victims at a single meal and there was nothing left to sit over. Naturally, I had seen myself as a hero who would rid the district of this terror. Alas, I was to be disappointed. When, at last, we did find the remains of a human kill, and I sat over the grisly bait, nervously perched on a shaky bamboo platform in a nearby tree, the tiger failed to make an entrance. Eventually, we injected the corpse with strychnine, and that was the end of the man-eater.

About this time I invested in my first car which was, in some ways, a more frightening adventure. The car was a 'T' model Ford and had to be collected from the north bank on the other side of the Brahmaputra which, in places, was five miles wide. I had driven before, but not a 'T' model Ford, which worked more like a tractor than a car and had a unique system of gear control. The gears were operated by foot and the accelerator was a lever on the steering column. One position of the foot pedal connected a forward, another the reverse gear, and there was very little margin between the two. By the time I had reached the ferry steamer I had acquired some measure of control over this weird machine, but driving up two planks set steeply at an acute angle was sheer hell. If I wavered, I was likely to find myself in reverse and shooting backwards to my doom. In desperation, I would accelerate wildly and finish up rocketing across the deck. Somehow, I got on and off again, on the far bank, not into the river.

The car was a great boon and would go anywhere in all weathers. During the rains the roads resembled ploughed fields, but I would wedge down the foot lever with a block of wood and churn my way through the mud for hours in bottom gear. Once the engine got so hot that the floor boards burst into flames, and once I decoked the engine myself and, after reassembling it, found myself with a boxful of assorted leftovers — nuts, bolts and screws.

The old car went just as well without them. I have driven Ford cars ever since with pleasure, but none of the newer models have had the staying power of my old faithful.

Towards the end of the cold weather, I was sent to Sibsagar, a subdivisional headquarters of the Sibsagar District and once the capital of the Ahom Kingdom. It was a small town, built round what in India is known as a tank — a large artificial and rectangular piece of water bounded by a high bank. At one side was an ancient Hindu temple, administered by saffron-robed priests. Outside the town was the *Hathi Garh,* or Elephant House, a weathered brick building in which elephants, rhinoceroses and tigers once fought one another for the entertainment of the Ahom rajahs. Opposite the temple was the thatched circuit house, which I was to share with a young Anglo-Indian policeman, that is to say a Eurasian. The term, Anglo-Indian, used to describe a Britisher living in India but in my time, long before the European Economic Community was thought of, we usually called ourselves Europeans. The policeman was an amiable fellow whose Indian father was a hight court judge of good family, and his mother a Frenchwoman, so I suppose he was really a Franco-Indian. Having been educated at an English public school, he found it difficult to adjust to a society in which Anglo-Indians, who usually valued their white more than their coloured blood, were little respected by either race.

My policeman friend, having flown his own light plane from India to England, quite an achievement in the 1920s, had won a certain amount of respect and was by no means unpopular.

Later, during the rains, without the comfort of electric fans, we cooled our drinks in wicker baskets, enmeshed in water-soaked straw and hung from the veranda ceiling, where the breeze evaporated the water and cooled the bottles. The tank was holy, and could not be used for bathing, but there appeared to be no taboo against boating which was, perhaps, not surprising as there were no boats. What we did have were two bath tubs, each inscribed with the ubiquitous PWD. In these, clad in pyjamas, was set sail one torrid night, under a full moon, only to come to grief as the tubs filled with water and sank irretrievably beneath us. As every article in the bungalow had to be strictly accounted for, and 'foundered at sea' did not appear to be a satisfactory explanation for their disappearance, the PWD not being noted for its sense of humour, we had to scour the bazaar for two identical tubs and forge the PWD mark upon them. By such childish means we whiled away the time and managed to remain comparatively sane. But, during my visit to Sibsagar, I had a task to perform which nearly drove me round the bend.

Timber from the forests was not felled and converted by the forest department but by timber merchants, who paid royalty and took our permits for a given number of trees. The local beat officer then marked the trees to be felled, placing hammer marks and a serial number on two blazes on each tree, so that when the tree was felled one mark remained on the stump, the other on the bole. When the bole was logged, each log was similarly marked and its measurements recorded in a notebook. This complicated procedure was necessary because, unfortunately, by no means all timber merchants were honest, and many forest subordinates could be bribed. If a tree were to be found felled without a mark, it could be assumed that the felling had been illegal. If the quantity of timber removed from one tree exceeded what could reasonably have been converted from between the stump and the 'top and lop' left on the ground, it was a safe bet that the subordinate had obligingly included in the one entry, timber from two trees — one legally and one illegally felled. To make deception even more difficult, all sawn timber was similarly marked and accounted for.

On this occasion, a large number of unmarked stumps had been found in the working area of one timber merchant, and there were obvious grounds for believing that they had been felled illegally in collusion with the beat officer. My job was to check all the measurements in the forest, compare them with the records, and estimate how much timber had come from illegally marked trees. Then, to check the timber merchant's depot and discover just how much converted timber it contained. My records had to be such that they would stand up as evidence in a court of law, which was difficult when the sweat was running down my arms, and the pages of my notebook were soaking wet. However, in due course, this Herculean task was completed and in due course, too, because of some point of law, or further corruption, or possibly both, the defendant was acquitted.

The only interesting occurrence during this enquiry was a hailstorm, which heralded in the rains with hail stones as big as golf balls that went through the corrugated iron roof under which we were sheltering, and killed a tiger in the jungle outside.

While making my check, I stayed at a bug-ridden *dak* bungalow, the local public staging-house, near the village railway station. It was also near the bazaar, and I was serenaded each night by scavenging jackals and by the nasal and monotonous songs and beating of drums which is the music of India. An oil mill stood in the village, and what air there was was heavy with the sickly scent of oil cake. In the morning, having at last dropped off to sleep, I was awakened by the ejaculatory mouth cleansing of the villagers as they performed their toilet. It was an unattractive place but was not without interest.

People of numerous races walked the streets and haggled in the shops — Nagas returning to the hills, Nepali sawyers in jodhpurs, tea garden coolies from central India, and the Bengali babus with large holes in their suspendered socks, clutching their white dhotis * to keep them out of the mud. There were bands of Mishmi cane cutters, about to return to their village in some remote part of the Himalayas. They were a strange stocky people who wore a curious selection of clothes, heavy silver ornaments and fur caps on top of their long tangled locks, while at their sides hung swords decorated with yaks' hair. They were also extremely dirty and smelt strongly — quite the hippies of the jungle. Under a banyan tree sat a naked, ash-covered *sadu*‡, either fast asleep or deep in thought.

Lolling on cushions in their open-fronted shops were the banian shop keepers, usually fat men with pink pugarees on their heads and cold, greedy eyes. No doubt they were often good husbands and kind parents but they were also money lenders who charged exorbitant rates of interest to the peasants and held them in thrall for the rest of their lives. It was, I regret to say, the reformed British land system, which had made it possible to buy and sell land, that had unintentionally made this iniquity also possible.

The following cold weather, I moved to a forest bungalow in the same area, where a tea garden bordered the jungle, to supervise work in one of our forest plantations. Unaccountably, I contracted mumps and was moved to the tea garden assistant's bungalow, where the garden doctor attended me in his more sober moments. Like most of his kind, my kindly host was a Scot who had been a ship's engineer before joining the tea company. He was in charge of the factory where, during the rains, he worked the clock round, tending the machines which bruised the leaf and the ovens that dried it.

The tea plant, *Camella Sinensis,* is an evergreen shrub which is grown in neat rows below the shade of a light tree canopy, and covers an extensive acreage in Assam. Most of this tea is of the dark and coarse Assam variety, the finer and lighter-coloured kind having been imported from China, before the indigenous plant was discovered at the beginning of the 19th century. The foliage — two leaves and a bud — is picked by women coolies in colourful saris, who carry it in baskets on their heads to the depots. Then it is moved in bulk, sometimes by tramway, to the factory. Plucking goes on throughout the rainy season, and everyone heaves a sigh of relief when it is over.

* every-day dress
‡ holy man

When I had recovered from the mumps, I called on the manager's wife and was offered a drink, but when a servant appeared with the tray, it was covered with white mice. These creatures were apparently the lady's great joy and were brought to her every evening, much as children in some well-to-do families are brought to the drawing-room for a brief spell with their mothers. Having extracted a mouse from up my sleeve, I decided that the children would have been preferable.

My dislike of the manager and his wife was not entirely due to their mice — they were not very nice people. Once a week, the local planters' club opened its doors to the members who arrived from far and near to drown their sorrows, forget the frustrations of the rainy season, and acquire a hangover. The women, under the watchful eye of the burramem, talked scandal in the ladies' room. The men did their gossiping in the billiard room and at the bar, one end of which was reserved for the burrasahibs, their assistants being confined to what was, presumably, the lower end.

It was not my business to criticise this ancient though inane convention but, in my opinion, the husband of the mouse lady went much too far and theirs was one of the few planters' bungalows which did not remain on my visiting list. It so happened that once a month the local dentist paid a visit to the club, in order to torment his patients. On one such occasion, my host, the assistant, had raging toothache. His boss owned a car but my host did not, and so was in the habit of riding the ten miles to the club on his pony. It might be imagined that the manager would have offered his assistant a lift, at least on this occasion, particularly as he had to pass his subordinate's bungalow, but not a bit of it. The great man and his lady drove to the club in reasonable comfort while my friend, with his throbbing tooth, trailed behind on his nag. If I remember aright, the assistant did eventually give his boss a good hiding, which was probably worth it, even though he lost his job. Fortunately, however, this was not a fair sample of tea garden life — the tea industry had its archaic and absurd social conventions but the managers were usually decent and kindly men.

The planters were also extremely hospitable, that is as far as fellow Europeans were concerned — they had even less social contact with the Indians than the officials. Indians were debarred from membership of the European clubs, and could only attend as honorary members if sufficiently important. Naturally, the Indians resented this discrimination but it was, I think, to some extent understandable. To the European, a club was a place where he could relax with his friends after spending what was often a frustrating day with his Indian brothers. The average Britisher looked forward to an evening with his own kind and in his own kind of world. He wanted to enjoy an atmosphere as near to that of home as possible, where he did not have to watch his tongue for fear of unintentionally giving offence, and where, in fact, he could put his feet up and let his hair down. The Indians felt slighted, but their homes were usually just as exclusive as the European clubs. Their women were often in purdah or too shy to meet Europeans; few Indians, who could do so, brought their wives and daughters to the clubs, and their only contact with our world was the occasional hen-party at home.

As far as the garden labour force was concerned, there was no social contact at all between the Europeans and Indians. The labour force, with the exception of a few babus, consisted of jungle coolies, with whom the management, of whatever colour, would have been unlikely to have any common denominator. The garden manager was still something of a paternal despot: the coolies, as long as they kept their place, were well cared for. Most managers made a point of getting to know their coolies and understand them. If they had any complaint, they appealed to the burrasahib, and labour relations were usually good.

The coolies came to Assam as indentured labour from the poorer parts of India and were paid what, according to local standards, were high wages. They had good houses, and each family was allotted a plot of land. Each garden had its own school, hospital and doctor babu. Each company had its European doctor. Many of the coolies remained on the garden when their contracts were completed. But, the coolies were taught to know their place. Woe betide any coolie or babu who kept his umbrella up when passing a European, or who rode his bicycle past the burrasahib's bungalow.

From Sibsagar I was sent to Gauhati where, during the following rainy season, I was placed in charge of the range office, and learned to do accounts, fill in returns, and take evasive action over awkward files. I soon discovered that goats, given half a chance, devour paper and could be relied upon to get rid of any unwanted correspondence. If the goats failed, there were always the white ants.

For some reason the division was being run at the time from Shillong, and I had the use of the divisional officer's bungalow, delightfully situated on the bank of the Brahmaputra. The coloured sails of country boats would appear over the garden hedge, and my cook used to fish out of the cookhouse window. There was the story of a previous cook, who had done the same thing, and tied the line to his big toe while he busied himself with his master's dinner. He unfortunately hooked a very big fish, which pulled him through the window and he was never seen again.

The *Durga Puja* came round once more, and I spent it in camp, further up the river with an old planter and another youngster, where we fished and shot jungle fowl. The planter was a rum old boy. When I first entered his sitting-room, I found each chair covered with a board, each board being pierced with nails which pointed menacingly upwards. I was relieved to discover that this was to discourage dogs, not visitors.

The old man, who was fond of his booze, had been warned by his doctor not to drink too much alcohol, and had been rationed to one glass of whisky and soda a day. He got over this by filling his tumbler full to the brim with whisky at sundown, and adding soda as the evening progressed and the level of the liquid fell.

Soon after returning from this camp to Gauhati, I learnt that I was to take charge of the Garro Hills division and prepared for my departure, elated at the thought of at last being able to run my own show.

CHAPTER 3

Bamboo Country

TO REACH TURA, the district headquarters in the Garo Hills, was something of an undertaking. There were three roads into the hills but their surfaces tended to get washed away during the rains and they had not yet been repaired. As a result, I had to sell my trusty Ford and start the journey by steamer, which proved to be a slow but pleasant form of transport. The sandbanks in the Brahmaputra are far from stable, and each rainy season shift their position, appearing again in unexpected places. Although the leadsman took repeated soundings from the prow, it was not long before we were firmly aground in the middle of the river, and remained there for some hours until we were pulled off by another steamer. At night we usually tied up at a ghat — one of the river jetties — and loaded cargo, a noisy and sleep-denying process as heavy objects were thrown on to the deck with deafening precision.

When not tied up, we sailed at night by the beam of a powerful searchlight, in front of which were soon collected the corpses of millions of insects in a pile several feet high. During the day we were surrounded by a picturesque medley of shipping. Country boats, large craft in which the crew and their families lived in barrel-shaped cabins under bamboo matting, sailed downstream before the wind, or were laboriously towed upstream by members of the crew, heads bent in long line along the river bank. Dugout canoes crossed from one bank to the other, and fishermen, wading in the shallows, cast their nets into the water. In midstream, men lived for days on huge rafts of simul logs as they drifted down the river to the match factory at Dhubri, at a deceptively fast speed. At a later date, I was to go after one of these rafts in a canoe to check the raftsmen's timber permit. It took only a few minutes to overtake the raft but, by the time we had done so, we were several miles downstream and were lucky to get a tow back again.

After disembarking from our steamer at Mankichar we climbed into a lorry and travelled for a few miles along a slippery road. Then my kit was transferred to a bullock cart which ploughed through the mud at two miles an hour while we walked impatiently ahead. When we finally arrived at Tura, little more than a village, with its empty streets, I felt I had reached the back of beyond as, indeed, I had, and for months the only fellow-countrymen

I was to see were touring officials. The only Europeans stationed in the district, using the term European rather loosely, were the American Baptist missionaries and two Italian priests, the two missions competing for souls of the pagan Garos in a markedly disunited manner. The Roman Catholics were making more headway at the time because the Garo is addicted to rice beer and the Italians enjoyed a nip, whereas the Baptists were strict teetotallers.

The Americans were a devout and kindly couple who lived in a comfortable bungalow insulated from the world by mosquito netting, and took their vacations in the United States. They gave tennis parties and refreshed their few guests with coffee and doughnuts. The Italians lived in a bare and uncomfortable shack and spent most of their time in the villages, where they ate native food and earned a stipend of thirty rupees, or £2.25 a month.

The Deputy Commissioner was an Indian noted for his anti-British feelings, and his assistant an Anglo-Indian who hated his guts. Later we were to have a European D C with an Indian assistant who, although an ardent nationalist, entertained no loathing for the ruling race. I used to dine with the assistant at his bungalow, where we sat on the floor before a huge dish piled high with rice, which we ate with our fingers as we talked politics. I sometimes feel that, if there had been more rice-eaters among the British, there might have been a more lasting partnership between the two races. We were a tight little community of aliens which kept to itself and had little social contact with the local people. Our relationship with the Indians was too much that of the prefects with the lower-fourth, one which hardly recommended itself to a people with an older culture than our own.

When I arrived at Tura I had yet to meet these characters and discover its mildly disturbing undercurrents. I was much more interested in the magnificent view over miles of hilly country. I have always loved the hills and the fresh, cool air was a delight after a rainy season in the hot, airless and steamy plains.

My bungalow was a wooden building built on an exposed spur and, as usual, on stilts. After positioning my few sticks of furniture, I was sitting at ease in a comfortable cane chair after supper when I was surprised and somewhat alarmed to see the carpet suddenly rise several inches in the air. This phenomenon, I was to discover, was caused by the wind whistling through the floor boards. But I should not have been surprised at a supernatural explanation because the Garo Hills have a strange, eerie character and are the home of numerous spirits.

The hill folk of Assam are mostly animists, who do their best to placate these spirits but, even though these people can be weaned from their primitive superstitions, the spirits are less easily exorcised — at any rate one still feels they are around. I have no first-hand experience of the supernatural but can tell one authenticated story. In the Naga Hills is an inspection bungalow with two rooms, one of which is haunted. The Deputy Commissioner had experienced the haunting and, being an anthropologist with an inquiring mind and wishing to see how others reacted, was in the habit of surreptitiously allotting the haunted room to those who toured the hills in his company. All these people had the same unpleasant experience. This took the form of a dream in which, crawling towards them along a narrow passage, was a baby with a monstrously deformed head, surrounded by an aura of evil. Just before the apparition reached the dreamer he would wake up in a cold sweat. The only explanation I can offer is that the haunted room was said to have been built on top of an old sacrificial stone and that the sacrificial victims were probably human.

I was told this story by the Deputy Commissioner and by a friend of his, both of whom had experienced the dream and both of whom were doctors of science and, presumably, reliable witnesses. Whatever the true explanation, strange things certainly took place in the hills. One of the dreamers mentioned above once witnessed a trial by ordeal in which the accused, being apparently unaffected by intense heat, was duly acquitted of his alleged crime. He assures me he was not dreaming at the time.

The Garos did not appear to find their environment oppressive and were a cheerful people, whom I found to be congenial neighbours. I cannot witness to the spiritual state of the Christians but, if cleanliness be next to godliness, the missions had accomplished something. In my opinion, the missionaries went too far in supressing old traditions and associations, something which would have earned the disapproval of the wise Gregory the Great, but the Christian Garos were sober, cleaner and possibly happier members of society than their pagan cousins. There were, it is true, some less praiseworthy characters among the converted but this was to be expected when those who had lost 'caste' in their own community for some misdemeanour, embraced the Christian faith solely, one suspects, to find a new niche in society.

During the cold weather I bought another second-hand Ford of a slightly more recent vintage, but most of my touring in the hills was on foot along the mountain tracks. Sometimes my kit was carried by elephants, sometimes in pointed baskets on the backs of coolies. Most of these journeys were through bamboo country which, from above, looked like a giant's cornfield. The tree forest had mostly been destroyed by generations of *jumiers,* what was left having been reserved by the Forest Department. The commonest tree was sal, a gregarious fire-resistant species. It has a bulbous, carrot-like root, which grows thicker each year until, even though the stem may be burnt back, a stage is reached when sufficient energy has been stored up in the root for it to send out a strong enough shoot to withstand the fire. In grassy areas we made use of this characteristic to establish new sal forests, and evolved an 'early burning' technique which has spread to other parts of India and, I am told, to Africa. The grassland was burnt in the cold weather, early in the morning, when the dew was on the ground, thus preventing a fierce fire, and, after a few years of such treatment, the sal was in control. Sal also seeded beneath the bamboos and, by judiciously thinning the culms, the weeds could still be kept in check, while the sal seedlings were able to establish themselves in the shade of the clump.

India is not an easy country to describe because, apart from the colours, it is the smell of the place that gets you — the pungent odour of elephant dung, the scent of burnt grass in the hot weather, pine trees in Shillong, the smell of decay in a forest swamp, and the sickly, soporific, often beautiful, sometimes overpowering smell of the vegetation. The Garo Hills smelt of bamboo. Not only did they grow everywhere, sometimes in clumps, sometimes singly, but they were used by everybody for everything. Houses were built entirely of bamboo — bamboo poles supported the buildings, and walls, roofs, doors, floors, window shutters, shelves, tables and beds were all made of woven bamboo matting, tied in place with strips of bamboo. Water was carried and rice cooked in hollow sections of bamboo, divided below a solid node which formed the bottom of a tubular container. Bamboo shoots were considered a delicacy by both elephants and humans. Bows, arrows and spears were made of bamboo.

In more 'civilised' places the flattened kerosene tin is used to cover the roofs, and the tins themselves are used as water vessels, but in most Garo villages the ubiquitous bamboo was still man's, and woman's, best friend.

The bamboo matting was made by beating the culms flat, and then weaving them together. As one walked across a bamboo floor it tended to give slightly and crackled disturbingly beneath one's feet. Sometimes, if woven too loosely, the legs of one's chair would disappear through the matting and one would land with a bump on the floor. But then, of course, the Garos squat and their floors are not designed for chairs.

The rest houses, staged along the bridle paths at something like ten mile intervals, were clean and attractive when new, but the same could not be said of the sanitary arrangements — a seat made of three bamboos in the form of a triangle, over a hole known as the 'long drop', in a small hut at the far end of the compound. Each bungalow had its visitors' book complete with a remarks column, and in one an Indian visitor had written indignantly: 'This latrine is too far from bungalow'. Noting his remark during his travels, the hard-hearted commissioner had added helpfully: 'This officer should start earlier'.

When on tour, we would start early in the cool of the morning, arriving at the next bungalow around midday, and spend the afternoon inspecting whatever we had come to see. Normally, my cook had tiffin ready in next-to-no-time and, as soon as I had bathed and changed my clothes, an appetising meal would appear on the table. Given a hole in the ground and a piece of tin to cover it with, this genius could prepare a four-course dinner that would have done credit to many a restaurant, and in record time, too. Chicken soup, roast or curried chicken, sometimes venison or jungle fowl, potato chops* and vegetable marrow; caramel custard or banana fritters, were all within his repertoire. There was always plenty of fruit — oranges, bananas, pineapples, mangos, lichees or papaya, called pawpaw, I believe, in the West Indies. Once one had acquired a taste for it, there was the Garos' rice beer to wash everything down. Papaya is full of pepsin which prevents indigestion. If cooked with meat, it will make the toughest joint tender. My cook was also an excellent bread-maker, baking the bread in a tin covered with hot ashes — a welcome change from our staple diet of leathery, unleavened *chapatis.*

Sometimes between camps I left the bridle path and took a different route to the elephants along a village track. Hill folk know nothing about contoured roads and normally take the shortest route between two points, however steep the gradient. These paths were hard going, but saved time, and it was always interesting to follow less well-beaten tracks. Only once did the elephants and I lose one another, and I had to take refuge in a Garo village and subsist on a diet of bananas until we were reunited.

The Garos Hills were full of wild elephants, as well as bamboos, and it was here that Kipling's Little Toomai rode on the back of Kala Nag and saw what man never had seen before — the dance of the elephants. I never saw this dance. However, I can vouch for Kipling's fund of remarkably accurate information. As he says, wild elephants never appear to notice a man on another elephant's back and once I rode through a large herd with the wild elephants grazing peacefully all around me, sometimes almost within touch. There were sedate mums, chastising their squealing babies with sticks held firmly in their trunks, while others caressed their offspring fondly. Young bulls eyed one another suspiciously, and all around was the sound of snapping bamboo shoots and succulent chewing. Sometimes, for no apparent reason, a cow would let out a shrill scream but, by and large, it was a peaceful scene that I shall long remember with pleasure.

* Rissoles

Elephants are good mothers, and their calves remain with them for some time. It is not uncommon to see as many as three calves tagging along behind a cow, the older ones still getting an occasional suck at her teats, which, unlike those of most mammals, hang between her forelegs. Also unlike other animals, elephants often have help in bringing up their children, when 'auntie', an old barren cow, attaches herself to the family and acts as nurse.

On another less peaceful occasion, I followed a herd on foot. I was walking quietly up-wind and got quite close to the *hathis*, which is the Assamese name for elephants, who were moving with scarcely a sound. It has always amazed me how quietly these huge animals can push their way through the undergrowth. I was watching, with some amusement, a mother helping her calf up a steep bank by prodding its small backside with her knee, when the herd bull suddenly got wind of me. Wheeling in his tracks, he spread his ears and raised his trunk suspiciously, before slowly, silently and menacingly striding in my direction. I should, perhaps, explain that the herd bull, if he is with the herd, brings up the rear when his family is on the move, the leader being an old cow. This sounds rather like a general leading his army from behind but, as animals normally move up-wind, it is, I suppose, from the rear that the unexpected danger is likely to come.

Fortunately we were moving along a river bank at the time. Elephants are good swimmers and our departmental elephants frequently swam across the Brahmaputra with their mahouts on their backs, and only the top of their heads and the tips of their trunks out of the water. But this river was full of huge boulders, which I could cross by hopping from one to another, but which an elephant could not negotiate. As my job was to preserve elephants not to shoot them, I made a hasty crossing while the bull loudly challenged me from the other bank.

There is a belief among the Garos that their hills are the home of a pigmy strain of elephant, but I never found them. Nor did I ever discover one of the legendary elephant grave-yards, which are said to exist in the jungle, but which nobody has ever been able to find. Dead elephants are seldom seen, but the jungle covers a lot of ground. Elephants are also long-lived creatures, often reaching a hundred years or more in their natural state, so deaths are not particularly frequent. Moreover, wild animals seek solitude when they know their time has come, and wander off to some remote place, usually near water, to die alone. Elephants are, I believe, no exception, and the dead and dying elephants I have encountered have been in river beds.

It is amazing how quickly a corpse, even one as large as an elephant's can disappear in a hot climate. Vultures, jackals, tigers and porcupines make short work of the flesh, and what is left is eaten by ants and broken down by micro-organisms; the bones sink into the soft ground and, in one rainy season, undergrowth has covered the spot. It is far more likely that elephants meet death alone than that there are vast stores of ivory to be found in some elephant cemetery. It is true that numbers of dead elephants have been found in Africa in one place, but these are likely to have died together of some abnormal cause such as a rinderpest epidemic.

Elephants have few enemies apart from man; other animals, including deer, are less fortunate and the red dog is their constant and cruel foe. Packs of these beautiful but heartless animals were common in the Garo Hills and, although they have to eat, and hunt for a living, they cannot be called endearing creatures. These packs pursue their quarry sometimes for hours. When the hunted animal is exhausted and stands at bay, the dogs surround it in a snarling, slavering ring. Members of the pack dart in and out, some urinating in the quarry's eyes, and others tearing at its belly until, at last, it sinks to the ground, and the pack moves in. I once saw a fine Sambar stag meet his end in this way. When I arrived it was too late to save him, and the only consolation was that it was I not the dogs who ate his flesh.

The Sambar is India's largest deer, a magnificent animal four to five feet high at the shoulder which feeds at night and lies up during the day. These deer have an unmistakable bell-like call and for some reason, which as far as I know has never been satisfactorily explained, frequently have a bare patch on their necks. The barking deer are much smaller and, unlike the sambars whose hinds often graze together, live in pairs. Their alarm cry, which they delight in sometimes for no apparent reason, has earned them their name, and is a constant reminder of their presence. There is also a pigmy mouse deer in the Garo Hills that I have only seen once, and know very little about. There were, of course, tigers and leopards, but I was never aware of coming into close contact with these while in the Garo Hills, except on one occasion and then I did not realise the fact until afterwards. Returning home to camp one evening through the jungle, I was surprised to hear the sound of sawing not far from the path. Wondering who could be working so industriously at such a late hour, I pushed my way through the undergrowth in order to find out, but, although I beat about for some time, nobody appeared to be there and soon the noise stopped. Later I was to discover that this sawing noise is made by leopards.

Wild pig were common — large, black and extremely active creatures, they did a great deal of damage to the villagers' crops. The men had to sit up at night on bamboo platforms called machans to protect their paddy fields from the wild animals by means of an intricate arrangement of tin cans, which clanked and jangled as they pulled a series of strings. There were also bears, which were seldom seen, and the chattering monkeys who, uninhibited, hurled abuse, and sometimes other things, from the tree tops.

Monkeys are good swimmers but don't as a rule like getting their feet wet, and I once witnessed their crossing of quite a wide river by means of a monkey chain. One monkey anchored himself firmly to a tree on the river bank. The rest of the troop held hands, anchored themselves firmly to the first monkey and, hanging from the tree in a chain, began to swing. Eventually they achieved sufficient momentum to swing across the river and grab a branch on the far bank. Then the monkey anchored to the original tree let go and swung across on the other end of the chain. The whole operation was carried out smoothly and quickly, without any fuss, but sometimes monkeys did make mistakes and accidents did occur.

One day I came across a pathetic sight, a baby gibbon with its arms round the neck of its dead mother at the foot of a tree. The mother must have missed her hold or, possibly, seized a rotten branch and fallen to her death. I picked the little creature up, and it immediately put its tiny arms round my neck and made the appropriate baby noises. Deeply touched, I carried it home to my camp and succeeded in rearing it on condensed milk which it sucked from my handkerchief.

The babe turned out to be a male and had the white brow and loud voice of his tribe and soon his hooloo — hooloo was resounding from the tree tops in my compound. Hoolocks are, unfortunately, jealous creatures and cases are not unknown where pet ones have attacked their master's children. I had no family at the time but the gibbon is also a most destructive animal, and it was not long before he had destroyed the vegetables in my garden and stolen most of my smaller possessions. Fortunately, my head clerk had a liking for the young vandal and he went to a new home.

Life was less complicated without my pet but I missed his constant chatter and even his occasional tantrums. He had a friendly way of searching my hair for fleas, and his wizened little face could express all the human emotions. He was a comical figure, balanced by tiny hands at the end of long arms that stretched to the floor as he stood, or waved above his head as he walked unsteadily across the room. But once aloft in a tree, he was in his element, a picture of acrobatic perfection as he swung from branch to branch and sang hooloo, hooloo, hooloo in pure delight.

I suppose, if one went out of one's way to find it, there was danger to be had from the larger animals in the jungle. Certainly if one shot them and wounded, rather than killed, one's prey, then elephants, tigers and leopards could be dangerous, but if unmolested they usually made themselves scarce. It was the smaller creatures, the sort that stung or got under one's skin, that were the real pests — the pinging mosquitos, the horse flies, the stink bugs, which really did stink, and, particularly during the rains, the black, slimy and revolting bloodsuckers, the leeches.

If one stood for a few moments on a forest path these evil creatures would come looping towards one from all sides — agile, sinuous black worms with angry yellow streaks on their backs. Once gorged with blood, they turned into bloated and inert sausages nearly as big as a little finger. To protect ourselves against them, we wore boots with putties over our trousers. The natives smeared their bare legs with tobacco juice but, even so, half a dozen or so of these evil creatures usually got past our defences and took their toll of blood. The best way to get rid of them without leaving a nasty sore was to touch the brutes with the stem of a tobacco pipe when, allergic to nicotine, they would drop off immediately.

Anyone overtaken by nightfall in the jungle was in real trouble, and there are recorded cases of people losing their way and dying through loss of blood. There is also an even bigger and more horrific model, the elephant leech, which is an aquatic species. A friend of mine once ran his car off the road and became trapped under it in a pool of water. He was not seriously injured and managed to keep his head above the surface, but was so covered with these monstrous leeches that, had he not been rescued fairly quickly, he would certainly have died.

When actually benighted in the jungle, the safest course, if one could stomach the ants, was to sit in a tree. Alternatively, the leeches could be kept at bay by lighting a fire and surrounding oneself with a ring of wood ashes. I believe leeches subsist entirely on blood, and it has always puzzled me whose blood they suck when there are no humans around. Certainly they attack animals as well as people, but there are not so many of them, either, to the square mile, and there must be a leech to every square yard — no wonder they have good appetites.

Another persistent intruder was the tick, found mainly in grassland. As far as man was concerned, this was more of an irritant than a danger, but it could produce a nasty sore. The tick can, however, be death to dogs, which are liable to contract tick fever, and I lost two in the Garo Hills. If pulled forcibly away from the skin, a tick usually left his head behind, but a lighted cigarette end applied to the tick ensured a complete extraction. Hornets, soldier ants, and over-sized horse flies were menaces — I once pitched my tent on a hornets' nest on a river bank, and had to take to the water. The huge spiders, whose beautiful dewy webs sparkled in the morning sunshine, are, as far as I know, quite harmless, except to other insects.

The two dogs I lost died at the end of a long march through the hills one rainy season. I was on my way to Shillong for the month's recess we enjoyed each year, working in the Conservator's office, and getting rid of our prickly heat and prickly tempers. One dog, a mongrel, was mine, the other, an attractive spaniel called Jane, belonged to my chief, who was on leave. It was Jane who fell ill when we arrived at Gauhati. She was suffering from tick fever, and was in such a bad state that the Government veterinary officer advised leaving her at Gauhati in his care. She died soon afterwards, and my own dog fell fatally ill of the same disease soon after I had reached Shillong. I was filled with remorse, convincing myself, in spite of the death of my own dog, that she had died because she felt deserted, and would have recovered if she had accompanied me to Shillong. I just don't know; at the time, the important thing had seemed to be to place her under expert care as soon as possible, and the vet was a good man. Difficult decisions have, unfortunately, to be made all too often in life and, when things go wrong, one cannot help wondering if one did the right thing.

In addition to the fauna, much of the jungle flora had unpleasant characteristics, from the needle-sharp spines of the canes to the razor-sharp edges of some of the grasses. But the chief devil was the surat plant, a giant needle with a sting like an electric shock, which seared the flesh and could produce a high fever. The Ahom kings of Assam once used this nettle to beat their enemies, and I once knew a member of the Indian Civil Service who, when in the jungle, used its leaves in place of toilet paper, with disastrous results.

Perhaps I have painted too fearsome a picture of the Indian jungle, which I learnt to love, and which, once one knew one's way about and the precautions to take, was less frightening than the concrete jungle of 'civilisation'. It could be cruel but there was no unnecessary cruelty. If an animal killed, it was in order to eat, or to win a mate, and fights between rival males were seldom fatal. Deer were constantly on the look out for danger, as we are when we cross a busy road, but their nerves probably remain steadier than ours, and they do not, I feel sure, live in constant fear any more than we do.

Nature is also incredibly neat, and wastes nothing. She has an efficient and, on the whole, humane disposal system. We all have to die some day, and a sick animal or weakly babe is soon put out of its misery. In a world created by a loving God, pain and suffering are things that we find hard to understand, but there is probably less, and certainly no more, pain and suffering in the jungle than in so called civilised places.

The jungle also has its compensations, for instance the *pani lota,* a thick pipe-like liane full of pure, refreshing water. The forests with their hothouse atmosphere during the rainy season were oppressive, but they were filled with colourful orchids, and were the home of brilliantly coloured birds and butterflies. Although only the fit survived in it, the jungle possessed a wonderful sense of peace that I have found nowhere else except, perhaps, on a mountain. The Assam jungle is no garden of Eden but it has something which civilisation lacks, and can provide man with all his basic needs.

One of the range headquarters in the Garo Hills was at Baghmara in the south-east corner of the district, where the Someswari River disgorges into what was then the plain of Bengal. The forest range officer was an intelligent Sylheti, who was always turned-out immaculately in a spotless uniform, but who made the mistake of under estimating other people's intelligence. I once inspected one of his plantations that had just been planted, and stooped down to tug at one of the sal plants to make sure that it was firmly embedded in the ground. To my surprise, it came out of the ground quite easily being, in fact, not a rooted seedling but a twig cut from a branch. Apparently the range officer had run out of seedlings and, sooner than admit the fact, had hoped to fool me with these useless cuttings. Needless to say, I was furious and gave him a good dressing down. But my fury was later to be tempered with mercy because of his exemplary conduct in a dangerous situation for which I was to blame.

Close to the village was a cavern known as the Bats' Cave, which I decided to explore, and, armed with an electric torch and a couple of boxes of matches, the range officer and I entered a narrow passage lined with stalactites and stalagmites. The local Garos refused to come with us, and I had no intention of going very far, armed with such inadequate lighting.

The passage ended in a huge cavern where, apparently hanging in mid-air and at a considerable height, a pair of eyes, caught by the light of the torch, glared down at us. The eyes turned out to be those of a guisarp, or monitor lizard, a harmless reptile about eight feet long, which was sitting on top of an immense pile of bat droppings.

We cast around and, finding a narrow opening at one side of the cavern, decided to explore a little further. The opening led into a tunnel about five feet high, the roof of which was apparently lined with brown velvet. The velvet consisted of thousands of bats having an upside down siesta, who suddenly came to life and poured out of the passage with indignant squeaks. Bats must possess very efficient echo sounders because, as far as I can remember, not one flew in my face.

At the end of the passage was a small opening through which we managed to squeeze and, not being able to turn round, we went on. We crawled for some time along what was little more than a crack, and finally emerged down a slippery slope into another passage, the bed of a sizeable stream. As we found it impossible to get back into the crack, we waded downstream with the water up to our waists, in the hope that it would lead us into the open. Unfortunately, the stream disappeared down a hole, and it was at this stage that I dropped the torch into the water — the light went out and refused to go on again. Luckily, the matches were safe and dry in my shirt pocket and by their light we discovered yet another tunnel. We groped our way along this, hitting our heads on various sharp pieces of rock in the dark until we emerged into what seemed to be a large cave, and sat exhausted. We hadn't a clue where we were but seemed to have been heading more or less in the right direction, and hoped we were somewhere near our point of entry, but the matches were finished and further progress impossible. All that was left to us was prayer, and a rather faint hope that our prayers might be answered.

The Garos who had guided us to the cave were waiting outside its entrance, at least we hoped they were, but, if we called to them, there seemed little likelihood that they would hear us. However, there was nothing else we could do and so we yelled lustily. At last there came an answering and, we felt, mocking echo, faint and seemingly far away, but when we called again it appeared to be louder. Then the light of a torch flickered against the rock wall of our tomb — the Garos had arrived in answer to our call. In fact, we discovered we were sitting in the same cavern which we had first entered, with our friend the guisarp still on his smelly throne. We were glad to say goodbye to the bats and their cave, and to feel the sun on our faces again.

At Someswari the roar of the river, as it plunges over the rapids, is always in one's ears — thunderous in the vicinity of the rapids and dying to a murmur in the distance. The river craft were dugout canoes made from logs of wood, which had been laboriously hollowed out with fire and knife. Being light, they could easily be dragged upstream through the rapids. Shooting the rapids in the opposite direction was an exciting and exhilarating pastime for which a fine sense of balance was needed.

The river was full of mighty mahseer and I spent some exciting hours spinning for the big carp below the rapids. My rod was a strong greenheart, and the bait a spoon about two inches long, which was cast across and downstream and wound in against the current. If taken by a big fish he would dash off at speed with the line screaming. At last his mad rush would end, and the line could be wound in again until he took control and dashed off once more. The important thing was to keep the line tight and to lower the point of the rod when he leapt out of the water. It could take half-an-hour or more to land a big fish. As often as not he would get away at the last moment.

Spinning for mahseer is an exciting sport, but the Garos have their own method of fishing, which probably requires more skill, and is as old as it is interesting. The biggest fish lay in a deep pool under overhanging rocks, and the Garos would float past in a dugout while one of them dived down through the water and harpooned his fish with a spear. The fish would move off, but the spear was attached to a float at the end of a line. The men in the canoe would race after the float as it was dragged along by the fleeing fish, catch hold of it and haul him in.

Large numbers of fish were also caught with the aid of poisons extracted from plants. The poison had a stupefying effect on the fish, which became unconscious and floated on the surface, where they could easily be collected. Such fishing was illegal but was frequently practised with good effect.

Another place, which I was able to reach by car, was at the foot of the hills on the Bengal border. The Bengalis of the Mynensing district, who had been converted to the true faith of Allah by their Mogul conquerors, were a dark-skinned, pugnacious people. They were short of land and frequently encroached on that of the Garos, and it was in this connection that I made my last visit. Unfortunately, I developed a bad bout of malaria. This was during the hot weather before the break of the rainy season, and running a high temperature under canvas in such circumstances did not auger well for a rapid recovery. In between bouts of fever, I decided to make for home and, feeling weak and shaky, started up my old car and set off along the bumpy road.

For a time all went well, the car bounced along the dirt track, slithered round hairpin bends, and raced along level stretches at 20 miles an hour. Sometimes the hillside dropped almost sheer below us for hundreds of feet, but in my fevered and light-headed condition, this did not seem to matter very much, and I broke into song as the car lurched from side to side.

We were about half way home when we had a puncture, and about three-quarters of the way when the second tyre burst. It would have taken hours to get hold of another tyre from Tura, so we continued to bump along on the rim. The final straw was when we ran out of petrol. All the fuel I had was a little in a pressure lamp, and a two gallon tin of kerosene. There was enough petrol in the lamp to fill the carburettor and start the car, then we hastily topped up with kerosene and completed the journey, the engine knocking furiously, and the exhaust polluting the environment with clouds of black smoke.

In those days, the bitter taste of quinine was seldom out of my mouth. As a prophylactic, we took five grains religiously every evening but, even so, we got malaria. The dose was then thirty grains a day for the first week, twenty for the second, ten for the third and five for the fourth. If one's digestion could stand this sort of thing, one naturally recovered, but there was always the chance of malaria developing into blackwater fever, which could be fatal. As I was getting far too many attacks, and had done four years in Assam, I decided to apply for some home leave, in spite of the fact that this would be a cold weather one.

My brother was farming at the time in the south of England and had spare stabling to offer. I invested my savings in a horse, and had a season's hunting in Berkshire. Presumably, one must store up heat in one's bones because, while other people were going about muffled up to the ears, I hardly felt the cold. Fifteen years later my blood must have got thinner because, when I finally left India, I found the English winters almost unbearable and would still be glad to give them a miss.

CHAPTER 4

A Mixed Bag

WHEN I RETURNED from leave I was posted to Nowgong, which lies on a flat plain surrounded by paddy fields, a forgotten place, bypassed by the mainstream of life. The district, however, offered some of the best shooting in Assam, which is to say in India, most of which was to be found in savanna country covered with tall grass and a sprinkling of trees — an ideal habitat for game. There was also deciduous forest and, between the Naga and Mikir Hills, a huge block of tropical evergreen forest, said to be the largest remaining area of forest in India. Assam must be one of the few places where such forest is found outside the tropics, and the Nowgong district probably the only place where, due to a freak micro-climate, areas with annual rainfalls as low as 43 inches, and as high as 64 inches, almost touch. Except for this low rainfall area, which is the driest in Assam, ecologists believe tropical evergreen to be the climax formation for this part of India. Most of the deciduous forest and the pine forest on the hills, the bamboo and grassland, are thought to owe their existence to biotic and edaphic factors, such as the burning of the jungle by man and the grazing of domestic animals.

Both the Assam-Bengal Railway and the Assam trunk road passed through Nowgong, which lies between Gauhati and Jorhat but, only thirty-seven years before I arrived in the country, Assam had no railways, and the proposed line was being surveyed.

Mrs F. S. Wilde accompanied her husband on this pioneering venture and wrote an account of her experiences in 1892. The party travelled by tonga from Shillong to Nowgong, having reached Assam by river steamer. Some four marches from Nowgong, the roads ceased to be recognisable as such, and it was necessary to plough through dense grass eight to eleven feet high and, later, to cut a way through almost deserted tree forest. The Wildes called their camps names like 'Nightmare' and 'Pea Soup', the latter referring to the water supply. Of the eight Europeans mentioned by Mrs Wilde, three died of malaria and one, her husband, was eventually murdered. Most of the high grass is still there, or was in my day, and neither the jungle nor the condition of the roads was very different, but the single track railway line was a memorial to those brave people.

When I arrived at Nowgong, I found my bungalow had been gutted by fire and that the new building was not yet completed. To start with, I shared a bungalow with my friend, the Anglo-Indian flying policeman, who was now Superintendent of Police at Nowgong. The bungalow, which had been condemned twenty years before, had whitewashed cow-dung plastered walls and a thatched roof, which was a haven for small mammals and reptiles. It was built on a river bank and, when the river rose, as it frequently did during the rains, we had to drive or wade to it through six inches of water. In the hot, humid conditions of the rainy season, our books became mildewed and fungi grew on our shoes; we stood the legs of tables and cupboards in tins of water to keep the white ants at bay.

My own bungalow, when I got into it, was at least modern, but there was no electricity and therefore no electric fans or refrigerators in the station. All we had to cool the atmosphere were pull punkahs — pieces of cloth hanging on frames suspended from the ceiling, which were pulled backwards and forwards by a rope, which passed through a hole in the wall. The punkah-wallah, who as often as not went to sleep, sat outside in the compound. It was impossible to get anybody to pull a punkah at night, when it was most needed. Blind punkah-wallahs were said to be the best because they couldn't tell the difference between night and day. Sugar, sprinkled round a sleeping punkah-wallah, was said to attract ants and keep him awake, but this was something I never tried. When I was unable to sleep because of the heat, and got sick of tossing and turning on my bed, I would get up and go for a spin in my car. In those days, car windscreens were made to open, and an open windscreen in a moving car was more effective than any fan — it was heaven to feel the cool air against my sweating body. Once, when I had not used the car for some days, a swarm of bees settled in the stuffing in the back of the rear seat. As the car moved off, they began to hum angrily and I had to put my foot down until the last bee had been blown out of the car.

There was a small planting district, with a planters' club, at Salona, about twenty miles from Nowgong. The club opened once a week and for a ten rupee subscription (fifteen shillings in those days, or 75p) one had the use of the club house with its bar, billiard room, card room, a rather primitive nine-hole golf course, a couple of tennis courts and a polo ground. Polo originated in the nearby state of Manipur, and Assam polo must have been the cheapest in the world. As a member of the Assam Valley Light Horse, the local territorial regiment, I was paid a horse allowance of thirty rupees a month, which was half the cost of keeping a polo pony, and with one pony I could expect to play a couple of chukkahs of scratch polo each club day. My mount was an Australian Whaler called Toke, but he spent more time carrying me about the jungle than he did playing polo.

The weekly club nights, patronised by planters who were usually denied one another's company for six days in the week, tended to be uproarious affairs, and it was usually well after midnight before we got home. When we did, our servants were dutifully waiting to serve dinner with all its four courses and we did our best not to disappoint them.

The road to the club was a narrow one on an embankment above the paddy fields. One night I was being driven home by another member of the club when we were held up for the umpteenth time by a string of bullock carts. Eventually, my driver stopped the car, jumped out and went to the head of the line, as I thought to clear the road. Instead he turned the first cart round and the others, unbeknown to their sleeping drivers, followed suit along the way they had come. Then he jumped back into the car and away we sped. I was trying to decided whose conduct was the most reprehensible, that of the bullock cart drivers or the trickster, when we went into a skid. Completely out of control, the car was about to plunge into the paddy fields when the driver wrenched the wheel round and we returned to the centre of the road. We passed a convoy of bullock carts with some difficulty, and, eventually, saw a building ahead which, half asleep as I was, I took to be my bungalow. When we got out, we found we were back at the club — without our knowing it, the car had completely turned round in its tracks and we had been hoist with our own petard.

My first encounter with an elephant in the Nowgong district was near the Salona club, and it was a very dead one. One night at the club, I was told that somebody had shot an elephant, and the next morning went to investigate. The Assam planters, once they accepted you, were the most friendly and hospitable people, but they were not particularly well-disposed towards officialdom. I was a bit surprised that they had been so eager to draw my attention to an apparent case of poaching. At the time I had had the feeling that I was being excluded from some joke, and the following morning I discovered what it was. The elephant, which had reached an advanced stage of decomposition, was lying in deep water between the high banks of a river. I reluctantly agreed with the planters that, as the governmental official responsible for elephant control, it was my job to remove this one and preserve the purity of the water supply. I didn't quite know how this was to be done, but felt I had been put on my metal and was determined to manage it somehow.

Removing over four tons of decomposing elephant from the bottom of a river bed is quite a job, and it took three days. First we had to cut a ramp through the bank to the water's edge, and then rope, haul and coax the huge carcase onto dry land. As it had reached the stage when it was almost ready to fall apart, this was difficult, and the smell terrible — a few minutes at a time was all I could bear to spend in the company of the dead animal. We got rid of the putrid pachyderm in the end, but it was some days before I ceased to smell. When I visited the club, even my best friends retreated to the other end of the bar and left me in no doubt as to the reason for my unpopularity.

My second elephant encounter was with a *goonda,* that is to say a rogue, who, at the time of our meeting, was very much alive and had been causing havoc in a village, breaking into storehouses and eating the villagers' rice. Elephants were preserved by the Government, but gentlemen of this sort had to be dealt with, and the only way to do so was with a bullet. Elephants usually become rogues either because they have been wounded or have been expelled from the herd by a stronger bull and are, as a result, in a bad temper. Others may be suffering from toothache, but whatever the cause, once they have killed their man, they tend to lose their fear and kill again.

Killer rogues were proclaimed with a price on their heads. This one was not yet a killer, although he was making a confounded nuisance of himself. To deal with his ilk, a new control scheme had recently been introduced, which allowed approved sportsmen to shoot them, under certain conditions, even though they had not been proclaimed. Male Indian elephants are of two kinds, tuskers and *maknas,* the latter possessing only short tushes and, in Assam, the *makhnas* were in the majority. To make sure that both were kept under control, a tusker could only be shot after a *makhna* had been accounted for. I had to shoot several solitary males while serving in Assam, but they were all *makhnas* and I never secured a pair of tusks. No doubt I could have done this if I had really wanted the tusks, but I never did like shooting elephants, and only did so in the course of duty.

This particular elephant, the first I ever shot, was looting grain in a village in the North Cachar Hills, which separate Nowgong from the Surma Valley and the district of Cachar. The railway line, originally surveyed by Mr Wilde, crosses these hills, and the elephant was operating in a village near a railway station called Hathikhali*. Mr Wilde and Mr Peddle, one of his assistants, lay buried in lonely graves a few miles away.

I spent the night at the Hathikhali inspection bungalow and set off early the next morning with two shikaris‡ from the village through fairly thick undergrowth. After a little, we kept stopping to listen and eventually heard the sound of snapping bamboos not far away. Elephants have poor sight but

* hathi khali means elephant enclosure
‡ hunters

excellent hearing and a powerful sense of smell. They are not difficult to approach up wind, as long as one does so quietly. In this case, the *goonda* was accompanied by a smaller bull, which is not unusual. Guided by the noise they were making, we were almost on top of them before we were aware of the fact.

Elephants are large animals, superficially all of one colour and, one would imagine, easy enough to spot. In reality, there are slight variations in their colour schemes, and this is accentuated by the fact that their backs are often plastered with mud. In thick jungle the huge bulk of an elephant tones in to a remarkable extent with the light and shade of its surroundings and, until it moves, the animal is almost invisible. When they do move, these huge creatures can glide through the jungle without a sound.

My guide suddenly laid his hand on my shoulder and pointed ahead. I peered into the shadows without at first seeing a thing. Then the elephant moved slightly and, like a picture puzzle, suddenly came to life. Luckily, I saw both elephants, or in my innocence might have shot the wrong one.

The elephants were standing in a mud hole about thirty yards away throwing muddy water over their backs. At close quarters, shot at the correct angle with a suitable weapon (mine was a double barrelled 400-450, high velocity rifle) an elephant is not difficult to kill. There are four lethal shots, three into the brain and one into the heart. Standing on the ground, one can shoot into the base of the bump on the animal's forehead, or from the side take the heart shot. Again, one can aim for the brain standing to one side and slightly to the rear of one's target. The target, in this case, is the hollow behind the eye, in which a mahout places his knee when sitting on an elephant's back. The fourth shot is from the rear into the base of the skull, and should be taken from a point slightly above the elephant.

The *goonda* was standing sideways-on, and I had to wait until he moved slightly away from me so that I could shoot into the brain at the correct angle. I dared not move myself, for fear of making a noise. The target circumference for this shot is about the size of the end of a tin of fifty cigarettes, in which we used to buy our smokes. It was not a difficult shot at short range, providing the elephant kept still and the man with the rifle kept his nerve. This was my first elephant, however, and my heart was pounding like a sledgehammer and my hand shaking like the proverbial reed.

It seemed a long time before the huge animal moved into the right position. I took a deep breath and, fortunately, a steady aim, and pressed the trigger. The elephant crashed to the ground stone dead and his small companion disappeared into the jungle with a series of shrill trumpet blasts. I fired some more rounds into the huge bulk to make sure that the elephant was dead, and then sat down feeling limp and empty as one does after narrowly avoiding a motor accident. The fore feet of the elephant had a circumference of four feet ten inches, which gave a height at the shoulder of approximately nine feet eight inches, or twice the circumference of the foot. The bigger Indian elephants measure between ten and eleven feet in height to the shoulder, so this was one of the bigger ones. I had done my duty and saved the villagers' paddy, but once the elephant was dead I got no further satisfaction out of it. As I looked at the huge pile of flesh, over which the ants were already beginning to crawl, I could only feel a sense of waste, and regret at having ended the life of such a magnificent animal.

The section of the railway that crossed the hills to the Surma Valley, left the main line at Lumding Junction, the railway headquarters in Assam, which was later to become famous as the Manipur Road Base, the main forward base for supplying the troops in the Burma campaign. In a brick bungalow at Lumding, which could have been built by nobody but a railway engineer, lived two European friends of mine, a railway official and his wife. When they were not in their bungalow at Lumding, they travelled up and down the line in a comfortable saloon coach, which was rather like living in a caravan, and were able to call in at any station they wished to visit. As Lumding was also one of the my range headquarters, we saw quite a lot of one another.

Twice, I spent my annual holiday with this couple in the Sikhim Himalayas which, to any one who loves the hills, is as near as they are likely to get to paradise in this world. We took these holidays at the end of a hot and sticky rainy season and the contrast between the snowy uplands and the sweltering plains was all the more appreciated.

At Siliguri, at the foot of the Himalayas, passengers left the train and transferred either to the mountain railway or a car. Both the road and railway line climbed steeply round a succession of hairpin bends, so sharply that the engine of the train almost met the guard's van at the back as it twisted and turned.

Darjeeling, nestling among the pine trees, was not unlike Shillong, but was nearer the roof of the world than the Assam hill station. Beyond Darjeeling was the native state of Sikhim, a large tract of mountainous country with few roads, the gateway to Nepal and Tibet.

On our first holiday we travelled east to the Tibetan border, where the trade routes cross the Natu and Jelap Las into the forbidden country at around 12,000 feet. Both passes are above the permanent snow line, and we watched hairy yaks ploughing through the soft snow with bales of Tibetan wool on their backs. The second time, we went west to the Nepal border at the Sangalalia La. The mountain tracks are well serviced with bungalows every ten miles or so. We usually walked, with coolies carrying our kit. Sometimes we summoned up sufficient courage to ride Props, a white Bhutan pony who had a habit of walking on the outer edge of the track which, as likely as not, bordered a precipice. In charge was Nima Darje, a charming little Sherpa, who had been on one of the early Everest expeditions.

I have said that Sikhim was a hill lover's paradise but it was difficult country. Surely, even paradise would be dull, if everything were too easy.

People who have never climbed often find it hard to understand the attraction of mountaineering, and there were times when I began to wonder what they were, as we descended a thousand feet into a valley, only to climb even higher up the other side. Sometimes we did this two or three times in one day. But each night we slept at a higher altitude, and our reward came when, with the wind doing its best to blow us into central Asia, we clustered round a cairn and watched spellbound as range after range of snowy peaks disappeared before us into the distance. From Sikhim, Everest looks deceptively small and unimpressive. Kanchenjunga is magnificent, a fantastic wall of glittering ice, forever changing colour, and the most beautiful mountain I have seen.

It was worth the sweat and toil to get such views — even worth the mild attack of snow blindness I suffered through not wearing my dark glasses above the snow line. For three days I was in agony with my eyes seemingly filled with grit.

We also had something of a shock when we discovered that, at Sandakphu, the highest bungalow in Sikhim had been gutted by fire. At something like 14,000 feet above sea level, we had to sleep in a temporary and airy shack. At such an altitude, unacclimatised travellers are apt to lose their appetites. My two companions lost theirs but mine remained unimpaired, and I ate fourteen sausages for supper. A recent World sausage eating record is thirty in seven minutes forty-nine seconds, but fourteen at 14,000 feet wasn't bad going.

Sikhim is full of saffron-robed Buddhist monks, *gumpas* and *chortens*. *Gumpas* are temples, usually adorned with flags, and *chortens* are stone monuments. The temples are sometimes fitted out with wind or water mills, which are also prayer wheels, and this is the only place I know where prayer has been automated. One may be excused a smile at such mechanical aids along the road to Nirvana, but they were of secondary importance. The Mahayana Buddhists of Tibet sought enlightenment for the sake of others and spent long years on the road in meditation, prayer and the attainment of mental and spiritual discipline. Few mystics can have found a more inspiring place in which to commune with the Infinite.

Buddhism was originally a reform movement within Hinduism. At first sight, the two religions have little in common — Buddhism a philosophico-religious system and Hindu polytheism with its elaborate temple worship, greatly concerned with sex and fertility, a disproportionate veneration of cows, and a rigid caste system, with the Brahmins at the top and the untouchables at the bottom. This popular religion of the Hindus, steeped in superstition, is however, only a part of the picture. From about 2,500 BC to 1,500 BC. India was occupied by the people of the Harappa civilisation, who were subsequently conquered by the barbarous Aryans. It was these newcomers from central Asia, who imposed their pantheon of gods and the caste system on the existing culture. The gods have multiplied but, during the Vedic age, the religion and philosophy of the two races was to merge, and a more spiritual monotheism evolved.

'In ancient times the gods of nature became convinved they were almighty. Spirit, understanding the mistaken notion of the gods, appeared,' is how the *Kena Upanished* explains the change. 'When they say, "sacrifice to this god" or "sacrifice to that god", these gods are but his (spirit's) manifestations; He is all these gods', affirms another of the *Upanishads.* These sacred books were written in the sixth century BC, at much the same time as the Greeks were slowly moving in the direction of monotheism — when Xenophanes wrote: 'There are many gods according to custom, but only one according to nature.'

Both Hindus and Buddhists, to whom all life is sacred, believe in the transmigration of the soul and in the final merging of the individual with the absolute. Both have their mystics who attempt to reach Nirvana by meditation and the control of the mind. As the Vedic sage explains: 'He (the seeker) shall meditate on Brahman (the universal spirit) with all aspects of the mind. This knowledge is found in austerity, self-control and meditation. It is supported by the Vedas and truth is its abode.' The worship of the Vedas is very different from the elaborate practice of the temples. Although there are fundamental differences in the beliefs of Christians, Hindus and Buddhists, yet each put forward a similar code of ethical behaviour. The *Mudaka Upanishad* describes Brahman as living in the heart. The beautiful *Bhagavas Gita* declares that 'He who is able to withstand the forces of desire and anger, even here on earth before he leaves the body, is a yogi, and a happy man. He who is happy within, who finds joy within, and whose light shineth within, that yogi attains Brahmanirvana and he becomes Brahmin' and again, 'He excels who looks equally upon lover, friend or foe; upon strangers, neutrals, foreigners and relatives; upon the virtuous as well as upon the sinner', a text which might also have been spoken on the mount in Galilee.

1   *John Rowntree*

2 *Setting off for camp*

3 *Ringing a tiger*

4 *Crossing Rajapara bheel*

5 *View of Brahmaputra from Gauhati bunga*

6 *Elephant at work*

7 *Joy on Punch*

8 *Local bus on bamboo bridge*

9 *Ford on mar boat*

10 *Adjutant bird*

11 *Swamp deer*

12 *Buffalo herd in Khasirunga Wildlife Sanctuary*

13 *Rhino*

14 *How one got on board*

17 *Family with Cook and Ayah*

15 *Baby elephant born in Kulsi camp*

16 *Sal forest*

19 *John with Peter*

20 *En route*

18 *A forest bungalow*

To the Buddhists, the wheel is the symbol of life, turned by the forces of greed, hatred and ignorance. Liberation from the wheel can only be achieved by those following the path of Buddha, which leads to Nirvana, a state of extinction and emptiness — Buddha's 'roaring silence'.

Not all Indians are saints, and many are doughty warriors, but both the Hindu and the Buddhist is normally a kindly, compassionate and civilised person who is less of a materialist than his more worldy Christian cousins in the West.

Unfortunately, I was unable to visit Sikhim in the spring when its rhododendron thickets were in flower. Instead, we enjoyed the music of the mountain streams as they raced over the boulders and crashed headlong over the waterfalls. Above the wooded valleys were the open uplands and, higher still, the rocky cliffs and snow slopes of the lower mountains; beyond were the great peaks — one of the places where man is brought down to his true size.

In case I have given the impression that life in India was all fun and games I hasten to add that it wasn't. Polo, *shikar* *, and mountaineering feature rather often because, in a country where there were no theatres or cinemas, few books or lending libraries, no television and only faint and crackly B B C radio programmes, sport was apt to fill much of one's spare time. In between, we did quite a lot of hard work.

Normally, when at headquarters, I worked from eight until ten in my bungalow, before attending the office from eleven until five. Instead of lunch, we ate a gargantuan meal called 'brunch' which, as its name suggests, was a mixture of breakfast and lunch. After office hours, I usually went for a ride, took the dog for a walk or played tennis and, if there was a club in the station, perhaps looked in afterwards for a rubber of bridge. Most of our tours of inspection took place in the cold weather when we travelled round the district inspecting offices and the work going on in the forest. Shorter and more uncomfortable tours were undertaken in the rainy season. A forest officer in India had to be a jack-of-all-trades — a road or house builder, a planter and converter of trees and a conserver of wild life. We were responsible for administering the forest and game laws, and for the welfare of the villagers living in the forest reserves. Sometimes I found myself inspecting a school or distributing medicine. If the accused in a forest case preferred to settle out of court, we were empowered to compound cases. Frequently, I sat under a banyan tree, dispensing justice. At all times we were accessible to anyone with a grievance and, if we were powerless to help, forwarded the

* Hunting, shooting

petition to the proper quarter or referred it back to the Conservator of Forests, who might refer it to the Government.

Sometimes a cold weather tour would continue for three weeks or more, and important official mail, known as *dak*, was forwarded in a canvas bag, carried by runner, to be dealt with in the evenings and returned in due course. As we had no clerical staff in camp, letters had to be laboriously drafted in longhand by the light of an oil lamp. Sometimes the *dak* bags were deceptively large. Once, when on tour with my chief, I received an extremely fat one, which impressed him greatly until the contents were disgorged and turned out to consist of four bread loaves and a bottle of whisky.

Naturally there was a good deal of delay in answering correspondence, which was kept down to a minimum as a result. And, because we were so often out of touch with higher authority, and usually had only an annual visit from the head of the department, we had to make our own decisions. This could lead to a pat on the back if they happened to be the right ones, and a rocket if they didn't. We tried out all kinds of experiments on our own initiative, which was fun, but if I was experimenting with some new planting technique I took good care to do so in some remote spot which nobody would discover if it proved to be a failure. The system encouraged personal initiative combined with a certain amount of guile.

During the rains working conditions were wet and uncomfortable, and the work was not always connected with forestry. Every year the Brahmaputra rose above its banks and flooded the valley. The river, perhaps a mile wide in the dry season, expanded to five miles during the monsoon and in a bad flood the water covered the low-lying country for some miles on either side. This was normally an occasion for rejoicing because the flood water spread fresh and fertile soil over the paddy fields and made the Assam Valley one of the most fertile parts of India. Occasionally, however, the floods were unusually severe, good soil was washed away and replaced by coarse silt and gravel, villages were cut off and houses sometimes submerged with considerable loss of animal and, occasionally, human life. Such a flood occurred while I was in charge of the Nowgong forest division and my policeman friend and I spent a hot and sweaty week touring the area in a country boat, delivering rice to marooned villagers and doing what we could to help them.

In the daytime we cruised around looking for marooned villagers, which was not a very pleasant experience. When it rained it was cool but wet and in between the heavy showers the water steamed in the heat and the sweat ran down our arms. At night we tied up in a backwater, where a piece of high ground had formed an island, and were pestered by mosquitos. Sometimes the bloated corpse of a bullock would float alongside in the dark, get wedged between the boat and the bank and fill the air with its noxious stench.

By day it was a strange and depressing sight to see water stretching to the horizon. Abandoned railway trains, which appeared to be standing in a few inches of water, were in reality perched on top of submerged embankments. When we ventured into the faster currents uprooted trees came rolling and surging towards us at an alarming speed; bits of houses, perhaps a solitary bedstead, and the occasional human corpse whirled past. Dogs and goats sat pathetically on small islands, domestic fowls clung to the branches of half submerged trees and the vultures hovered overhead, waiting for the water to subside. When it did, and the land reappeared above the surface, the corpses came to rest in the viscous mud.

Fortunately the water had risen fairly slowly, the majority of the villagers possessed boats and had managed to find sanctuary on the few remaining pieces of high ground. Many villages were built on such places and were marooned rather than submerged. Not many people were drowned but the damage to crops, animals, stores of grain and, in many cases, houses, had been considerable. The people were also living in great distress and under conditions ripe for an epidemic. The Deputy Commissioner, who was an Indian at the time, had things well in hand. Medical treatment was soon on the way and, fortunately, no further calamity occurred — within a few months the Brahmaputra Valley was back to normal. In the meantime, our mission was to feed the hungry. But, instead of being hailed as saviours we were often criticised for the quality of our rice which, we were told, was not fit to eat and would poison anyone who attempted to do so. It was, in fact, a perfectly good sample and, if not of the very best quality, the best obtainable at short notice. We eventually got rid of it but some villagers preferred to remain hungry rather than eat what we had to offer. Instead of being sustained by a glow of righteousness we returned home feeling deflated and somewhat cynical.

At this time the Congress party was not particularly active, but it was in the Nowgong District that I first made the acquaintance of the followers of Gandhi, the wizened little man, who seemed to have been forgotten by 1971 when India was at war with Pakistan. In the nineteen-thirties and 'forties his name was one to be conjured with.

Saint, political opportunist, prevaricator; Gandhi has been called all three. Many would claim, undoubtedly a saint, but whether he was an impractical idealist has yet to be proved. The Mahatma, the great exponent of ahimsa, or non-violence, believed that what he saw as the truth must be followed at all costs until, in the words of Professor Toynbee: 'Violence annihilates itself and leaves gentleness alone in the field'. But he was also an astute politician.

He believed 'that moral principles have no meaning unless they can be made to serve as guides of conduct in the daily affairs of men', and non-violent non-co-operation became the main weapon in the fight for Indian independence.

At the outbreak of hostilities in 1914 Gandhi had not yet become a pacifist, and he supported the policy of all out co-operation with the British in the war against Germany. In 1917 Dominion status had been declared as the goal for India but, within a year or so, repressive measures were being used, not only against extremist agitators, but politically-minded Indians who expressed liberal views. This led to riots, culminating in the shooting of unarmed civilians under General Dyer at Amritsar. In 1939 India was being asked to co-operate in a new war but, to many Indians, Dominion status seemed no nearer.

The Congress party resigned from the Government because it considered that India was being involved in a war which was no concern of the Indian people and about which they had not been consulted. As a pacifist, Gandhi has been criticised as a hypocrite for offering the British moral support in return for independence. His reply was that 'Even a non-violent person is bound, when the occasion arises, to say which side is just', and that he could not be expected to offer even moral support unless Britain made it clear, this time, that she meant what she said when she claimed she was fighting for the rights of democracy.

The Cripps mission, and a promise of Dominion status after the war, failed to break the deadlock — Congress was demanding independence immediately. In 1942 the British were told to quit India and Congress launched its non-violent civil disobedience campaign.

With the Japanese massing on the Indo-Burmese border, a civil disobedience campaign would have seriously interfered with the defence of India and the whole Allied strategy. It is perhaps not surprising that the Congress leaders and their lieutenants were locked up, but this left the field clear for more violent men to take over. The campaign, aggravated by toughs intent on loot and rape, ceased to be non-violent and for a few weeks, until suppressed by the military, the situation was extremely ugly in some parts of India.

If, as some people have claimed, Congress had planned an armed rebellion, they were extremely incompetent planners. The whole thing was over, and the situation normal, within a few weeks.

In Assam there were many members of the Congress party and Gandhi caps soon became fashionable. As an act of defiance, Congress supporters smoked *biris,* a small acrid kind of cheroot, instead of English cigarettes. In 1942 a number of staunch supporters of Gandhi found themselves in prison, and college youths made rude remarks, aimed at Europeans, as they passed them in the street. But there was little serious trouble in Assam, where the authorities succeeded in keeping things cool. Although there were some unpleasant situations there was, as far as I know, no loss of life. I was never involved personally, nor was there much bitterness evident on either side. The Assam Valley Light Horse, the local militia, showed the flag by riding through the countryside from time to time, but the police dealt with the trouble-makers without bloodshed, so all the troopers had was some healthy exercise.

Perhaps the fact that the Japanese were so near, and the Assamese had seen the pitiful state of the refugees, many of whom were Burmese, as they struggled into Assam, may have had its effect. After all, it was to suppress an invasion from Burma that the British had originally been invited to Assam.

It is, perhaps, of interest to record that, during my eighteen years in Assam, I never carried a defensive weapon, except on parade with the Light Horse, or for sporting purposes, and I seldom bothered to lock the door of my bungalow at night, even during these troublesome times. We were only once burgled, when we lost three or four small articles of little value.

To Gandhi, ahimsa, which he described as love in the Pauline sense, was an active, overriding spiritual force, and the only one that could defeat evil; a force which could, however, only arise in the absence of all hatred, and where there was a willingness to accept conscious suffering. He did not claim that passive resistance would save the life of the resister, but he was confident that, in the end, truth would prevail over what he saw as evil, and he opposed the use of force in any circumstances — even to defend his country from the Japanese invaders. He believed passionately that everything else would be added to him who sought the Kingdom of Heaven, even if it took several lifetimes to achieve this spiritual force.

Gandhi's philosophy, based on the centuries-old teaching of the Mahabharata and the Sermon on the Mount, was as far from being simply a political tool as it was from representing a vague moral principle. To the Mahatma it had become a way of life, and he considered it a human tragedy that people claiming to believe in the message of Jesus, the Prince of Peace, practised this belief so little in their lives.

It was, however, when Gandhi attempted to apply his philosophy to politics, and to use non-violence as a tool, that he ran into difficulties. Violence undoubtedly leads to the brutalisation of human nature and, as an ideal to strive for, non-violence cannot be called in question, but, it can be too easily discredited. It only needs the presence of a few hooligans to turn a non-violent demonstration into a massacre, which is what happened to a greater or lesser degree in India and, until the human race is less violently inclined, this seems to be inevitable.

To the average British administrator in India, engaged in a violent war, and believing that the military defeat of Hitler and the Japanese was the only way to save, not only his country, but civilisation and all that he held dear, Gandhi's was a puzzling philosophy. It was in fact, a philosophy that was misunderstood by many of Gandhi's own followers, some of whom looked upon ahimsa solely as a political weapon, which they attempted to use without the change of heart that Gandhi had insisted was a prequisite to success. As a result non-violence too often turned into violence and, on more than one occasion, the Mahatma called off the civil disobedience campaign as a result. In the end the saintly little man was assassinated by a fellow countryman, a fanatic who, like Judas, could not accept his master's gospel of brotherly love.

Some have claimed that India's independence was gained by non-violent civil disobedience. Others have argued that the comparative lack of violence enabled Britain to prolong her hold on the country, that it was only the war and the need to appease Congress at a time when India was under threat of invasion that eventually won her *Swaraj**. What the non-violent approach may well have done was to prevent all-out violent revolution with its inevitable aftermath of bitterness and hate, and so helped to cement that friendship between India and Britain which has lasted ever since independence was granted in 1947. That, after all, seems justification enough for Gandhi's philosophy.

The other main plank in this philosophy was Gandhi's attempt to encourage village industries, and his wish to see a spinning wheel turning in every peasant's home. He believed that an economy based on village industries had more to offer India than western technology and the doctrine of eternal growth. Certainly, machines have little relevance in a country with unlimited labour, and it would seem more sensible to bring industry to the villages rather than bring the peasants to the already over-crowded and squalid towns. Gandhi was, perhaps, chiefly concerned with the dignity of man but he also seems to have understood the economic needs of his country.

* Independence

CHAPTER 5

Shikar and Conservation

THE NOWGONG DISTRICT, as I have said, was a shikari's dream, abounding in both big and small game. I shot one of each principal species of the big ones — buffalo, bison, leopard, wild boar and crocodile, but the only tiger I ever shot was a cub.

For some reason, the Fates seemed to have decreed that, try as I might, I should not bag a tiger. Once I sat up over a kill and, just as the tiger appeared my mahout, either having got bored with waiting, or having misunderstood my instructions, arrived with his elephant to take me home. Naturally the tiger made off. Usually when a tiger kill was discovered, we sat at a safe height on a bamboo platform sited in a nearby tree. The platform, or machan, as it was called, was comfortable enough, but after sunset the mosquitoes were not. Tigers have an acute sense of hearing and it was essential to sit still and, as far as possible, without moving a muscle — a difficult thing to do when a mosquito is stabbing one's nose with its six sharp needles. One got into position before sunset, the familiar jungle sounds would gradually die away and, as night fell, one became submerged in a deep pool of silence. The slightest sound became amplified out of all proportion.

One day I came across a tiger kill and, as there was no one handy to build me a machan, climbed into a small tree and perched precariously on one of its branches. The tiger appeared in broad daylight and I had an excellent view of his wide head as he pushed his way silently through the undergrowth towards me. My first shot must have grazed the top of his head because he turned a somersault and then, still very much alive, bounded forward and stood listening just below me. At a range of about six feet I pressed the trigger of my rifle, the round in the second barrel misfired and the tiger bounded away, fortunately, in the opposite direction.

I shot the tiger cub by mistake for its mother. We were beating some high grass at the time, on elephants, and spotted the tigress slinking into a thick clump. As we drew nearer I could see a tawny patch filling a gap in the wall of grass and, thinking this was the tigress we had just seen, took aim and fired. Regrettably I discovered I had shot one of her cubs, which I had no idea existed.

I suppose most people have an inborn urge to hunt, and big game shooting can be both exciting and interesting, but animals are not always cleanly killed, however careful the hunter, and things happen that one regrets and which leave unhappy memories. I would, doubtless, have got my tiger sooner or later, had I persisted, but I soon lost the lust to kill and found animal watching more rewarding. I was beginning to take an interest in animal photography when the war started and films became scarce. Unfortunately, most of my stored negatives had become damaged by the damp when hostilities ended.

The last time I attempted to shoot one of these beautiful beasts I sat up with my wife at a place frequented by tigers. It was a bright afternoon and, when a tiger and tigress appeared, they created a striking picture in the sunshine. As usual they made a silent and sudden entry — one moment there was nothing to be seen but grass, the next there they were, every stripe clearly visible. The two animals started to play together like overgrown kittens, rolling one another over in the grass; the wish to shoot them disappeared never to return, and I am thankful to have taken away that happy picture instead of a tiger skin.

Small game were a different matter, being shot, as they were, for food. The occasional jungle fowl, pheasant or duck made a welcome addition to the pot and was a pleasant change from the eternal stringy, bantam-sized chickens which were our usual fare. The paddy fields were full of snipe and the *bheels,* or lakes, along the Brahmaputra, were covered with geese and ducks. Bar-headed geese, pochard, scaup, tufted duck and pintail gave excellent sport when flighting in the early morning and evening. The great brown Brahminy duck, or ruddy sheldrake, which mates for life, was immune from our fire.

We would rise at first cock's crow and get into position in good time. The sun, an enormous red ball would climb slowly into the sky and, as it appeared, the temperature would drop several degrees before it began to warm up again. Then, through the mist, would streak the first flight to be followed by another and another. With luck we would down a few birds and then return to camp for breakfast.

But it was not only the shooting that attracted us to the *bheels.* There were white storks with white, red and yellow legs, and whitey blue ones with pink legs; slow motion, grey herons and the grotesque Adjutant Bird, with a queer, flesh coloured lobe hanging below his beak and the look of a village idiot; there were graceful pink flamingoes and that talented fisherman the pelican. The latter drive the fish in line into the shallows, corner them and scoop them up with their great shovel-shaped beaks. Black cormorants sat immobile, seemingly for hours, with wings outspread. Kingfishers, pied and green headed, coots, moorhens, curlews, and plovers abounded. The most interesting of the small birds which lived in the tall grass was the Indian weaver bird, which weaves its nest of grass and hangs it from the stems of the reeds. Two of the most beautiful were the Golden Oriole and the crested Hoopoe, and one of the noisiest the Koel, the Indian cuckoo, whose monotonous cry heralds in the rainy season.

The Indian bird life was particularly attractive because it included so many of our British species. There were, for instance, the homely sparrows and the twit-click-clicking stonechat, as well as more exotic ones like the peafowl and the bee-eater. There were the great birds or prey like the eagles and the Brahminy kite and that repellent, but necessary scavenger, the vulture, but the Asiatic sparrow-hawk and the pale harrier too, were not unlike their European cousins. There were the great hornbills that seal their wives up in their nesting holes for the duration of the incubation period, leaving only a small opening through which to poke their food.

The other great attraction of this savanna country were the flowering trees which in the hot weather, when all else was dry and parched, enriched the landscape with their vivid colours. The Indian laburnum, really a cassia, carries pendulous chains of golden yellow flowers, and, later in the year, long pods which are pulped and used as a lazative. The same genus provides the senna pods with which the older generations among us were once all too familiar. The scarlet flowers of the flame of the forest were the most striking, and the cotton tree, or simul, with its orange flowers, was the most common. Its wood was made into matches and the white, cotton-like seed hairs were excellent for stuffing cushions.

Closer to the ground were the fragrant white flowers of the coffee family, the showy rose-purple blooms of the bauhinia, and the white clerodendron. What with the bright flowers, the gay plumage of the birds and the brilliant sunlight, it was a cheerful countryside before the sky was darkened by the monsoon clouds and the ground was turned into a quagmire.

The Nowgong district included a small game sanctuary at Laokhowa on the Brahmaputra, which was the home of a few Indian Rhinoceroses. There were many of these strange, archaic animals in the Kaziranga Reserve in the neighbouring Sibsabar Division and a few elsewhere. They were in danger of extinction and we did our best to preserve them. Unfortunately, in the East the horn of the rhino is considered of great value as an aphrodisiac and was worth something like its weight in gold. Poaching was rife and there was a brisk trade between India and China. Once when we seized such a horn and took the owner to court he proved that, far from being a genuine article, it was an ingenious imitation, so presumably the purchasers were sometimes cheated.

The poachers' usual method of capture was by a concealed pit, dug in a rhino track. Once in this, the animal was shot or, less humanely, speared to death. Unfortunately, although these pits were often discovered, the nature of the terrain and the high grass made it difficult for us to catch the culprits.

The Indian rhino weighs about four tons, much the same weight as an elephant. He is extremely solid and is covered with armour-plating. His single horn consists of modified hair loosely attached to the skin of his nose, and is of little use as an offensive weapon. His chief weapons are his razor sharp tushes, which he uses most effectively. In the heat of the day, he is usually found wallowing happily in a mud hole. At night he grazes in the open, and his tunnels riddle the grass which is from eight to ten feet high. Once when camping in the Laokhowa reserve, on the edge of a *bheel,* a rhino brought down my tent while I was asleep inside. Fortunately, he walked alongside it, merely breaking the guy ropes, and not through the centre, or I might nor be writing this now.

While in this camp I had another adventure, this time with an elephant. The reserve was surrounded by the cultivated land of both Mymensing immigrants and local Assamese. In order to gain more land, the Mymensingias did their utmost to intimidate the Assamese and drive them out of thir holdings. They also liked fish, which were plentiful in the *bheels* but which were let to leaseholders. The result was that the Mymensingias were constantly poaching the fish and were thoroughly disliked by my staff of forest guards, who were Assamese and only too eager to catch them at it. We laid an ambush and, after a free-for-all, rounded up about a dozen poachers but, having done so, the problem was to know how to deal with them. To reach the nearest police station, some miles away, they would have to pass through Mymensing territory, and I had only three men to look after them. In the end I lent my elephant rifle, without any ammunition, to the head guard and he successfully piloted the prisoners through the enemy lines. I, on the contrary, was left without a rifle, and was to have cause to regret the fact.

I was sitting in front of my tent on the edge of a *bheel* when the father of all *goonda* elephants appeared on the opposite bank. He was a magnificent sight, but I fervently hoped he would not approach any nearer. After a good hard look in my direction he turned aside and, without any show of unseemly haste, made a dignified exit in the direction of my two female baggage elephants. In accordance with the usual practice, the two cows had been turned loose to graze, each with a chain fastened to one of its hind legs. The chain, dragging behind the elephant, left a mark on the ground and made it easy to track the animal, which was free to go where it wished, until it was time to catch it again. The *goonda* obviously liked the look of the ladies who, judging by the ensuing conversation, must have found him equally attractive. As their squeals of delight began to fade into the distance I realised that they were being abducted and that it was time I did something about it. Although I had no rifle, I still had a shotgun and, as I could not afford to lose two valuable elephants, decided to give chase. It was easy to follow the tracks they had made through the grass, but visibility was practically nil and I did not dwell on the consequences should the *goonda* turn in his tracks and decide to see me off.

When I came up with the trio all I could see were bits of elephant showing through the grass, and had no idea which belonged to which. I decided to chance a shot in the air and trust to luck. Fortunately the *goonda* made off and the mahouts were able to recapture their charges, but I was glad when the forest guards returned with my rifle.

I had my pony, Toke, with me in camp and enjoyed some good gallops over the rice stubbles at the edge of the sanctuary. One day we jumped a fence, the pony caught his foot and we both turned a somersault and landed on our heads. I was completely knocked out. When I came to, I found myself back in the saddle with a large bump on my head and smoking a pipe — at least it was in my mouth. I knew who I was and that I was somewhere in Assam, but couldn't for the life of me remember where, which was a most peculiar and frustrating feeling. All I could do was to give Toke his head and let the intelligent animal take me home, which he promptly did. Strangely enough, the same thing happened to me while out with the Derwent Hunt, in Yorkshire, some years later.

I shot my buffalo outside the sanctuary but from the same camp. He was a fine bull standing up to his shoulders in the grass and I shot him at long range, aiming where I judged the heart would be. I realise now that this was something of a risky shot and, at the time, I thought I had missed the target. When I fired, the bull seemed to stagger but then gather himself together and charged straight at me. When he reached a few yards from where I was standing, he fell stone dead and, as I discovered afterwards, had been shot clean through the heart.

There are three kinds of deer which inhabit the grass country in Assam — the swamp deer and the hog deer, which we sometimes shot for the pot and, in the west of the province, a few herds of the beautiful spotted cheetal. The swamp deer, or *bara-sing,* meaning twelve horned, are not confined to swamps and their horns can carry up to twenty tines. In Assam they are often found in dry, grassy savanna as well as in swampy land. They live gregariously in herds and have a bray-like rutting call of 'ringhon' accompanied by a drone which F. W. Champion, a colleague of mine in India, has likened to the bagpipes. We found the swamp deer easy to approach on an elephant. The hog deer, being smaller, are more difficult to spot until the grass has been burnt in the spring and they emerge to crop the new growth.

The cheetal live in the sparsely tree-covered savanna land and numbers of them fall prey to leopards, seemingly to the unconcern of those that escape the attention of the big cats. Their colouring, strangely enough, would seem to have little protective value in open country, the spots resembling the patches of shade and light filtering through a tree canopy. Champion, who has seen far more cheetal than I, refers to their association with monkeys, the sharpest-eyed creatures in the jungle. The monkeys not only give warning of approaching danger, but also knock succulent fruits off the trees on which the deer feed. The cheetal is a good mother who, like many other animals, hides her young in the grass. The wild white cattle of Chillingham, in Northumberland do the same thing in the bracken.

Among the *Cervinae,* the cheetal is the elegant charmer, the sambar the solid and respectable citizen, and the barking and hog deer the gamines of the jungle.

The Nowgong district was noted for its elephants as well as for other species of game and, together with the neighbouring district of Sibsagar, was one of the main centres in Assam for elephant catching. During the season of 1945—46, just before I left the province, 289 elephants were captured, the following year 375.

Elephants have been captured in India for hundreds of years, but Assam is one of the few places in the peninsula where they still exist in any numbers. There was a time when every family who could afford to do so kept an elephant, and it was the custom to buy a baby elephant on the birth of a son and for the two to grow up together — rather like putting down a cellar of port. At one time elephants were used by the Indian army to carry guns, and gaily-decorated elephants have always been in great demand for religious processions and festivals of various kinds. The Indian princes maintained large numbers of elephants in their establishments and they were used extensively for timber work, transport and generally wherever power was needed. Nowadays there is still a limited demand but fewer people can afford to keep an elephant as a luxury and, anyhow, the motor car has replaced it as a status symbol. Better roads are making elephants redundant as transport animals, and tractors nowadays produce most of the mechanical power. In 1946, however, elephant catching was still of some importance.

Two methods of elephant catching are practised in Assam, *mela* and *khedda shikar*, or open and stockade hunting. In *mela shikar,* the professional elephant nooser, called the *phandi*, rides on the bare back of the *koonkie,* the trained hunting elephant, holding on to a rope, rather like a surf rider. Three or four elephants are engaged in the chase, which usually takes place in open country and results in small catches of the smaller animals. As I should have been very much in the way and might have endangered the success of the hunt, or even the lives of the hunters, I never took part in one of these hunts which must, surely, be one of the more exciting of activities.

In *khedda shikar*, the wild elephants are driven into a stockade, sometimes more than fifty at a time, the stockades being sited on elephant tracks, often in the vicinity of salt licks. In the latter case, the elephants come of their own accord to eat the mineral salts and clear their intestines of worms, which is usually done at the time of full moon. In the vicinity of a salt lick, the elephants are only driven in the final stage of their journey as they approach the stockade. In the former case, the herd is sometimes driven to the stockade over a distance of many miles.

The drive is accomplished by trackers who locate the herd and surround it on foot without the elephants suspecting their presence. They then move the herd slowly in the direction of the the stockade by tapping on trees, while the elephants continue to graze but slowly move away from the noise without being unduly alarmed. It may take several days before the herd reaches the stockade, from which walls of posts have been built on either side of the elephant track to form what is in effect a large funnel. As soon as the herd passes into its mouth, the men line up behind, beat drums and fire off their guns. The stampeded herd charges between the walls and into the stockade. As the elephants enter the enclosure, the gate keeper cuts the cane, with which the heavy gate is supported, and it bangs to.

Before the hunt starts, there is an important preliminary without which no elephant hunter would chance his arm. This is the sacrifice of a white cockerel to the spirit of the jungle.

The stockade, which is round and covers much the same area as a tennis court, is surrounded by a high palisade of posts and, inside the posts, by a ditch. Elephants cannot jump and the ditch is too deep and too wide for them to step across, but the bigger ones can lean over and press against the palisade with their heads. As, however, the posts, though bound together, are placed rather loosely in the ground, there is a certain amount of give and, however hard the elephants may push against them, they do not normally break. To discourage too vigorous an assault, there is a platform running around the outside of the stockade near its top, from which men armed with spears can fend off a breakout attempt.

While I was stationed at Nowgong, my mother and sister came out from England to pay me a visit and I took them with me into camp. We lived for a time in the grass huts which the Assamese call *bashas*, in a clearing in the forest and, one night, a large elephant walked through the camp between them. It must have been quite an alarming experience for my visitors although, accustomed as I was to such happenings, I did not realise this at the time. Their participation in an elephant *khedda* at the famous Soramari stockade was to prove even more thrilling.

The final drive into the stockade always takes place at night, and we arrived just as the herd was reaching the last stage of its journey. We climbed up onto the narrow platform surrounding the palisade. I had lent my 12-bore shotgun to the Anglo-Indian *khedda* officer so that the sound of the shots would help drive the elephants in the right direction, and we settled down to await events. He later returned the gun minus three inches of muzzle, which was rather sad as it was a valuable weapon. Apparently, he had tripped and fallen in some soft ground and, unknown to him the muzzle had become choked with mud. When he fired the gun the barrels luckily burst at the muzzle and not at the breech. Fortunately the gun was still serviceable after the end of the barrels had been sawn off.

We waited in tense silence, straining our ears to catch the sound of the approaching elephants. At last we heard the yells, drum beats and gunfire of the hunters. Something crashed through the undergrowth, and into the stockade strode a colossal and solitary *makhna*. As the gate fell to behind him, the monster raised his trunk, spread his ears and took stock of his surroundings with obvious displeasure. He then proceeded to batter the palisade with his broad head. Our companions on the narrow platform hurled abuse at the elephant and prodded him with their spears, while the Rowntree family clung for dear life to the rocking poles.

What had happened was that two male elephants had been mistaken for a small herd and, even when the hunters discovered their mistake, they felt honour bound to corral the largest of the two in honour of the visitors. This was, I fear, a rather unappreciated but heroic act which had demanded great skill and daring on their part. The elephant was, of course, too big to handle and was released as soon as possible, making a dignified exit through the stockade gate.

While I was in Assam elephant shikar was carried out by lease-holders, who tendered for their leases and subsequently worked under the supervision of the forest department. Some of these were well-to-do landowners, who themselves took an active part in the hunting. One of the most successful *mahalders*, or leaseholders, was an Assamese, Goramurija Goswami, who captured elephants to provide funds for a Hindu monastery of which he was the head. Later he became involved in politics and spent some time in prison on account of his connection with the civil disobedience campaign.

In the early days elephant catching involved a good deal of cruelty, the animals being kept for days in the stockade without food or water, until too weak to offer resistance, and many of them died. In 1920 Miroey, then in charge of the *kheddas,* introduced new rules which reduced the deaths from nearly 30 to under 5 per cent. The most important of these was that elephants must be removed from the stockade within four days of capture, and that each *koonkidar* must supply a *koonkie* to lead each capture to the training depot and see to its speedy training. Preliminary training was to be completed within two weeks or within a maximum of six weeks for very big elephants; the usual iron tipped spears were forbidden, and pregnant animals and those with suckled calves had to be released.

The elephants were removed from the stockade, roped to *koonkies* and, on arrival at the depot, were roped fore and aft between trees. To begin with, the ropes were stretched tight so that it was difficult for the animals to move, but each day, as they became more tractable, the ropes were eased until, by the time they had ceased to put up a fight, they were standing normally. The captives were fed rice, salt and grass or banana leaves, and were watered twice daily. After a day or two in captivity they were exercised each day, fastened by ropes, first between two and then alongside a single *koonkie,* with mahouts on their backs. Eventually they could be taken out alone, having learnt the essential words of command such as *bait,* the order to sit down. There was a famous case of a forest department elephant which escaped and after years in the wild was met by its former mahout who commanded *bait.* The elephant promptly sat down and the man got on its back and brought it home.

All the time the training is proceeding, the men are gaining the animals' confidence by talking to them, caressing them, singing them lullabies and feeding titbits as rewards. After each training session, the elephants are taken for a bath in the river and scrubbed with a brick. Gaining an animal's confidence is essential if it is to be trained and this implies kindness, not harsh words or hard blows.

Unavoidably elephants were sometimes injured in the rough and tumble of the hunt, and a full-time vet was employed by the forest department to treat the animals, which mostly suffered from bruised and sprained joints. We had no modern drugs or antibiotics in those days but the 'doctor babu' did wonders with the help of iodine; potassium permanganate, usually known as pinky pani, or pink water; olive oil, and even clay to plug the wounds. Our departmental elephants suffered chiefly from saddle galls caused by the pads on which we sat, and sometimes these developed into large abscesses. It always amazed me that the elephants allowed the doctor babu to incise these abscesses with his knife and syringe them out, and that he escaped the attention of their waving trunks.

The captured elephants were taken from Assam to the great annual elephant fairs in central India where they were sold, and I fear that, in spite of our previous care, some of them were neglected and did not live very long in the dry heat to which they were unaccustomed.

Elephant catching was, however, such an established business, and the elephants, such an important source of revenue, provided a living for so many people, and were in such great demand at that time, that to refuse to supply them would have been politically impossible, even had the powers-that-be wished to do so. It would have been equivalent to closing down the motor car industry in this country, and all we could do was to ensure that the catching and training was done humanely and to hope that our charges would enjoy as good a life as possible afterwards.

Unfortunately elephants are such avid feeders that they need large tracts of virgin jungle in which to live, and such tracts are becoming fewer and further apart every year. It is the opening up of the jungle for cultivation which is endangering the future of elephants and other wild animals more than anything else, and this is something which cannot be avoided. Fortunately, forestry in India is a paying concern and is smiled on by the local governments. There is a reasonable hope that the majority of the forest reserves, constituted as such in the time of the Raj, will continue to be preserved. When I left Assam in 1947 it contained 6,690 square miles of reserved forest, or 9.7 per cent of the total area; and 14.507 square miles of unreserved forest. No doubt much of the latter has since been disforested but, as far as I know, most of the reserves are still intact.

The forest reserves were, however, created to preserve the timber resources of the country and are not necessarily ideal habitats for wild animals, many of which prefer to live in the more open, sparsely tree-covered savanna areas. As a result, by 1947, 459 square miles of game sanctuaries had been established in the province, mostly riverside areas, subject to flooding and therefore not in such demand for cultivation. However, owing to the ever-increasing land shortage, there was a growing demand by cultivators for even these areas, and whether they can be preserved as game sanctuaries remains to be seen — fortunately there appears to be a good chance that they can.

In 1966 I received a heartening report from Mr. P. Barua, then chief conservator of forests in Assam, regarding the Kaziranga Game Sanctuary in the Sibsagar district, and the largest game reserve in the province. From this report it appeared that the area of the Assam game sanctuaries had actually risen from 458 square miles in 1947 to 580 square miles at that time. The annual number of visitors to the Kaziranga Sanctuary had increased from 192 to 3,723 within twenty years, the majority being Indians, with large contingents from the USA and Europe. The estimated number of rhino in Assam was 486, 400 of which were thought to be in Kaziranga where 366 were actually counted in 1965.

The estimate of rhino numbers in the Kaziranga Game Sanctuary was based on a detailed survey carried out by Mr. J. Julian Spillett, an American ecologist from the Johns Hopkins Institute, and the local divisional forest officer, Mr. H. K. Nath, on what are described as internationally approved lines. The high grass precluded the use of aeroplanes and an aerial count and, instead, the 166 square miles were divided into eight blocks, each block being again subdivided into sub-compartments of approximately five square miles, artificial boundary lines being cut through the grass where necessary. Eighteen parties, supplied with elephants, carried out the census over a period of two days, recording species and, as far as possible, the sex and approximate age of all the animals seen.

Apart from the rhino, there was a count of 349 elephants, 471 buffalo and over 1,600 deer, mostly hog deer but including a fair number of swamp deer and rather fewer sambar. The estimated total number of deer was 4,000 to 5,000. There were a few barking deer, wild pig were common and a number of otters were seen. Bison, tiger, bear and leopard were scarce, surprisingly so in the case of the carnivores, with so much game about. Sex and age were difficult to determine with some species but, in general, the distribution appeared to indicate a healthy state of affairs.

Elephant numbers were unexpectedly large, but burning of *jums* was going on in the nearby Mikir Hills at the time, and they may have sought refuge in the sanctuary as a result.

When I last visited Kaziranga in 1947, the only available accommodation was a two-roomed bungalow, furnished, but without services of any kind. From the nearest railway station a dirt track connected the sanctuary with the outside world. Today one can fly to Jorhat and from there travel the sixty miles to Kaziranga, over the well-surfaced National Highway in a comfortable bus. Arrived at the sanctuary, the visitor is accommodated in a modern, well-equipped tourist lodge administered by the Assam Tourist Department. The fans may not always work but I am told by a recent visitor that the food is good. A staff of over one hundred now guards the sanctuary and looks after the tourists, and thirteen elephants are provided for their use. I hope they don't all sit down together.

I am also glad to hear that a suggestion made by me when I was conservator, that the sanctuary should be used for scientific and educational purposes, has borne fruit. When the British left India most of us were afraid the game sanctuaries would soon be disforested but, I am glad to say, we were wrong. Kaziranga has proved to be Assam's biggest tourist attraction and its value as such is appreciated by the Assamese who, in these days of improved communications, are able to benefit from the tourists in a way that we never could.

I am told that the demand for land inside the sanctuary has tailed off, possibly because, since partition, no more immigrants have come in from Bengal, where land hunger is greater than among the Assamese. There is, however, an increased demand for grazing within the sanctuary. Within limits this might be a harmless activity, except that a grazier is always a potential poacher. There is also the risk of infection, which cannot be taken lightly.

Most of the graziers in Assam are Nepalies whose large herds of buffalo graze the grassland along the banks of the Brahmaputra. The buffalo milk is mostly made into ghee, or clarified butter, stored in old kerosene tins and sold in the towns. The domestic, but not so tame, buffalo cows frequently mate with wild bulls which visit them as they graze. This injects virile new blood into the herd, but the graziers' buffaloes are subject to rinderpest epidemics and the wild animals may become infected. The Government had a scheme for vaccinating the domestic herds and, if this were followed rigorously, perhaps the least-frequented parts of the sanctuary might be opened to grazing without any regrettable consequences.

Floods are an uncontrollable annual occurrence which cause some loss of animal life, but on the whole, probably do more good than harm by washing the *bheels* clear of the ever-persistent water hyacinth which would otherwise choke them up completely. Floods do, however, encourage animals to leave the sanctuary, which puts them in great danger from poachers. A proposed scheme to reserve a corridor between the sanctuary and the Mikir Hills, as an escape route, is worthy of further consideration.

The annual fires that sweep through the tinder dry grass during the hot weather preceding the rains are also unavoidable. Unless the graziers set fire to their grazing grounds, it is difficult for their animals to find succulent young grass, but these fires inevitably spread to the sanctuary. Fortunately, the sanctuary is criss-crossed by numerous *bheels* and swamps, and such fires are localised. Slow-moving reptiles such as the pythons may be destroyed but most of the animals escape the flames. The grazing of the wild herbivores is also improved and visitors to the sanctuary are able to get a better view of its inmates.

Poaching will continue to be a problem and the rhino will always be in danger as long as men worship at the shrine of Aphrodite Pandemos. In 1965, in spite of stringent precautions, eighteen rhino were known to have been killed by poachers, but this was a particularly bad year, only two having perished in 1966. Since then I have not heard how the rhino have fared but, all in all, the general picture appears to be encouraging and the future of wild life conservation in Assam seems to be reasonably well assured.

The one-horned Indian rhino is less aggressive than his African cousin but can, nevertheless, be a dangerous customer if annoyed. He is one of the few animals, apart from dogs and mice, that the Indian elephant really fears, and he can inflict appalling wounds to an elephant's undercarriage with his sharp tushes. At the same time, the Indian rhino is a remarkably easy animal to domesticate and in ancient times was used by the Assamese to draw their ploughs. While I was in Assam we caught three rhino in pits for the Regents Park Zoo. Unfortunately two died and, when one considers the hardship that wild animals inevitably suffer when in transit, it seems doubtful whether such transactions are justified. What was interesting was the rapidity with which these rhino lost their fear of man. Within a fortnight they became quite tame and I was able to enter the small stockade in which one of them was confined and handle the horny monster. Admittedly, these were young animals but were well past the calf stage being, in fact, the size of large bullocks. *Rhinoceros unicornis* is thick skinned, but his low IQ seems to have made him more rather than less tractable.

It would have seemed ridiculous at that time to suggest that tigers could ever become extinct, but in 1973 there were estimated to be only 2,000 tigers left in India, compared to 40,000 in 1930.

The concentration of species in the game reserves, as the surrounding jungle is opened up for cultivation, is likely to pose another problem, that of over-population, as it has in Africa.

This has already involved the culling of some animals, a necessary but unpleasant operation to the conservationist, and one which can scarcely be avoided in India. But, because elephants exist in communities and the members of a herd are interdependent on one another, the thinning out of each separate herd would so disrupt the elephant society as to lead to the eventual extinction of all the herds. This, at least, is the view of people who have studied the problem, and it is now felt that entire, selected herds may have to be destroyed, leaving the others intact — a grim task for those who have to carry it out.

In the meantime, I must congratulate the Government of Assam on its good sense in preserving this unique heritage, and long may it continue to do so.

Leopards used to be as numerous as tigers though one seldom saw them, but once I was uncomfortably close to one of these spotted cats. I was living under canvas at the time in a clearing in the sal forest and my dog, as usual, slept under the camp bed. One night his whining woke me up but, although I listened carefully, I could hear nothing, and crossly told him to shut up and let me go to sleep again. There was silence for some time and I was just dropping off when I heard a rustling under my bed — the dog beat a hurried retreat and started to growl angrily. My electric torch was under the pillow and, by its light, a spotted paw was revealed groping under the wall of the tent a few inches away. When I jumped out of bed, the leopard made off before I had time to snatch up a gun and give chase. The faithful hound apologised for the disturbance and I, for my part, felt rather mean for having been so mistrustful.

This was during the hot weather, often a time of violent winds and sudden storms. The next day I returned to camp in the afternoon to find a large tree lying across my tent. It is said that lightning never strikes twice in the same place but I felt that somehow I wasn't really welcome. I decided a nod was as good as a wink and moved to another site.

In some ways life in Nowgong was tough and unpleasant but it had many compensations and I shall never regret my three years in the district. My interest in wild life, which began with a rifle in my hands and ended with a camera, took me to many a place which I should never have visited in the course of duty. The same interest encouraged the forging of closer links with the jungle folk than would otherwise have been the case, and I am sure this is an essential part of a forester's training. I am also convinced that people who start out to shoot game usually end by becoming the most ardent conservationists. That was certainly so in my case.

It was on my last visit to Shillong from Nowgong that I met Joy Wingate, who became my wife. The following cold weather, she visited me with her sister and brother-in-law, Amy and Benjie White, with whom she was staying. We spent some time in camp where she decided she could stand the jungle life, as well as me, and we became engaged. We were to be married at home and sailed on the same ship, something considered rather daring in those days. This was a rather slow B & I steamer that called at Madras for cargo, where we had our first flight in a light plane which was taking people for trips. From Columbo we paid a visit to Kandy by train, and at Suez drove through the night to Cairo to see the pyramids and rejoin the ship at Port Said. The trip to the pyramids was on horseback, and not without incident. My wife-to-be's pony took the bit between its yellow teeth and galloped home at full speed disappearing in a cloud of dust over the horizon. Much to my relief I soon found Joy again, quite unharmed. Duly wed, we returned at the end of my leave to Kamrop District, where we were stationed at Gauhati.

CHAPTER 6

Peace and War

WE HAD TRAVELLED overland to Syracuse and from there taken a ship to Valletta, which was the roughest crossing I have ever made. Our small craft rolled and pitched incessantly and, by the time we reached Malta, both Joy and I had turned a sickly green and could scarcely stand. Malta is a bare, treeless place but, like St Paul, we were thankful to be on the island. Valletta is an attractive town, full of narrow streets and, at the time of our visit, drunken matelots.

We arrived at Gauhati after the long dusty journey across India and made our first home on the bank of the Brahmaputra as the cold weather was getting under way and the climate becoming bearable. The Public Works Department had given the walls of the bungalow a coat of fresh limewash and had painted the woodwork liberally with earth oil. In front was a raised portico which served as a car port, and on top, a veranda from which we had a splendid view of the river and its shipping and, beyond, the Himalayas. In the foreground was Peacock Island, with the dome of a Hindu temple just visible through the trees. I never discovered peacocks, but only monkeys on the island.

As the cold weather advanced the Brahmaputra shrank and the distance between Peacock Island and the mainland grew less until, by the end of the hot weather, only a narrow dividing channel remained. There was a belief that if this channel ever dried up completely it would mean the end of the British Raj. In some years it very nearly did, but whether one could walk dry shod to the island in 1947, Independence year, I don't know because I no longer lived in Gauhati at the time.

The Gauhati bungalow was the oddest I have ever encountered. A large house post dominated the centre of the sitting room, up which I always felt roses should be climbing, and the main bedroom overlooked the dining room, which was at a lower level. The upper half of the bedroom wall was open, and one could lean over and chat to people below. Anybody sitting in the veranda or climbing the steps to the front door had a clear view into the bedroom, unless screened by curtains. The bedroom was also connected by a door to my office, outside which usually queued a long line of petitioners who, one by one, were ushered into my presence. They did not, of course, approach through the bedroom, but there was little privacy for the lady of the house, and considerably less than a bride is apt to expect. However, it was a friendly place with a spacious garden full of palm trees, canas, balsam, morning glory and other colourful blooms and, often enough, other people's cows. We also had a number of hens which sometimes nested in the pigeon holes of my desk. I was once closeted in my office with the Conservator when one of the chickens shot out of its nest into the face of the great man. Even a fresh egg for his tea failed to restore our rapport.

The bungalow, which had a spare bedroom, was adequately furnished for the ridiculous sum of £100 with furniture made by a talented murderer in the local gaol. These were masterly pieces of work in unstained local bonsum wood, also known as Indian teak, the design having been meticulously copied from a Heal's catalogue. The curtains were printed locally at the Gauhati craft centre, with a tiger motif designed by my wife, and coconut matting provided an excellent depository for the dust which our sweeper swept under it. To complete our happy home there was Peter, my cocker spaniel, and Bogy, a black cat whose family, three black and three white kittens, arrived just before our first child. Our daughter, Jacqueline, was born at the local mission hospital. I got into trouble for prodding her from time to time as she lay in her cot, but this was solely due to fatherly concern on my part — she was so quiet I just wanted to make sure that she was still with us. We also acquired two country ponies — small hill tats of about 13 hands, but as strong as most horses. One, Toby, was a Bhutia and the other, Punch, a Manipuri* stallion. When, later, war work precluded such a leisurely form of transport and we had to part with the ponies, Punch went to a planter who trained him to stand while he shot birds, deer and, I believe, leopards from his back. Our most unwelcome guests were the cockroaches which swarmed over the floor and, when stepped on, exploded with a disgusting pop.

At Gauhati we acquired a domestic staff of nine, which may sound a lot, but Indian servants are members of the strongest of all trade unions. Each member of our staff had his or her allotted task and would never dream of doing any one else's except, perhaps, in camp where it was impossible to take them all with us. As the master climbed the ladder of promotion, he was expected, not necessarily to pay higher wages, but to employ more and more servants. There was our Mugh cook, Mamu, a Buddhist and a vegetarian, who seemed to have no objection to cooking our meat dishes; the *Khitmagar*, or butler, and my cook bearer who accompanied me on tour. There was that general dog's body, the *pani* walla, who carried water but also washed dishes,

* Bhutia and Manipuri are place names

if possible with a greasy rag which he carried wound round his sweaty neck. There was the Untouchable sweeper, who brushed the floors and emptied the commodes, and the *mali* who was the gardener. The undisputed ruler of the establishment was the children's ayah, Hidon, usually known as Mai, which means mother — a solid, dependable, no-nonsense Khasi woman, devoted to the children. Later when we had three children we employed two ayahs, but the ponies did better, each having its own syce, or groom. I also had two official orderlies, called *chaprasies,* whose function it was to run errands and carry messages, when they were not playing dice or sleeping under a tree. Each servant had his or her own little house in the compound.

At this time Gauhati had quite a large official European population and was the headquarters of both a judge and a commissioner who presided over several administrative districts each with a deputy commissioner, or DC, in charge. We had our own club, and a church where the government chaplain from Shillong occasionally preached. The club had two grass tennis courts and, later, I designed a golf course on what had been a rifle range. As a result, the course was rather narrow and could only accommodate six holes. However, we managed to play nine by using three of them twice, a practice which added considerable spice to the game, as one never knew from which direction a ball might appear. In addition to the officials, there was a large American mission in the station with its medical staff, and the Imperial Tobacco Company bungalow which housed its local sales manager. Gauhati was also an overnight stop for departmental heads from Shillong, about to tour the province.

The day usually began with a ride before breakfast and ended with tennis, followed by bridge or snooker at the club. A number of us also did a good deal of entertaining, and we dined frequently in one another's bungalows. Sometimes, when the guests were numerous, our crockery and cutlery proved inadequate, but the servants invariably managed to cope successfully with any short-comings. The guests were as likely as not to find themselves eating off their own plates and admiring their own garden blooms in the centre of the table. The Imperial Tobacco Company dinner parties usually continued into the small hours. I don't know how the custom arose, but we were young and nobody liked to break up the party. It usually ended with the guests and their hosts asleep on the floor — Morpheus rather than Bacchus having brought the festivities to a close.

Mrs Commissioner was a lady of the old school, and her dinner parties were more sedate. There were no croquet hoops on the lawn but one felt there should have been. The civil surgeon's bungalow also had its own mystique, but of a different kind. When I first came to know Gauhati and dined at the doctor's. I had occasion to seek the lavatory after dinner, took the wrong turning and pandemonium was suddenly let loose as devils or angels, I knew not which, whirled round my head; the air was filled with the beating of wings and with strange croaking sounds. It was only when I managed to find the light switch that I discovered I was standing in the centre of a hen house surrounded by startled hens whose house was an otherwise unused room in the bungalow. Another danger-spot was the Doctor Sahib's sitting room. Suspended from the ceiling, in the middle of the room, was a mysterious black bag which, like Pandora's box, was better left alone. It was, in fact, a mosquito trap, into the open mouth of which the unsuspecting insects crept during the day. A pull on a string then closed the mouth of the bag until such time as the mosquitoes could be destroyed. When I first saw it I naturally pulled the string, the mouth of the bag opened and I was enveloped in a cloud of pinging, biting anopheles.

Although Gauhati was the port of entry, so to speak, into Assam, most travellers passed through on their way between Calcutta and Shillong or to districts further up the valley. Occasionally, however, they stayed overnight, and sometimes we had unusual visitors, one of which was a tiger that had, presumably, been washed up by a flood. The pug marks of the large cat were clearly traceable through our compound, and the unfortunate animal was eventually shot in the local baker's shop.

The Kamrup district, of which Gauhati was the headquarters, extended to both banks of the river. The North Bank had a character all its own — a vast, remote stretch of flat, ageless land between the sandbanks of the Brahmaputra and the Himalayan foothills. It was a strange place, where the rivers dried up in the hot weather or suddenly disappeared under ground. Sometimes in camp we had to dig for water, which was so dirty that it had to be cleaned by dropping alum into the bucket to precipitate the mud. There were numerous *bheels* replete with wildfowl, peafowl strutted through the grass and, in the Manas Sanctuary bordering the Himalayan state of Bhutan, were a few rhino. The rivers were full of mahseer, and their banks a favourite site for the Governor's Christmas camps, which it was my task to build, and for which I sometimes received a polite letter of thanks from the great man.

This was the home of the Assam cheetal, and it was here that I once witnessed the delightful sight of a she sloth-bear carrying her cuddlesome cub on her back. Right in the middle of the wilds, a European and his wife had leased a piece of land from the forest department with a view to growing simul trees for the nearby match factory. They had rigged up miles of electric fencing in an attempt to keep out the deer, but with little success as far as the deer were concerned — they just jumped over it. On the other hand, never having met an an electric fence before, I received the full treatment. I am afraid their enterprise was in no sense a very profitable one.

During the cold weather the North Bank was delightful. In the rainy season it was a hot bed of malaria and was best avoided. Travel at this time of year could also pose problems. The rivers were in flood and the bamboo bridges erected at the start of the cold weather were soon washed away. These bridges swayed and creaked alarmingly under a passing car, but were immensely strong and extremely useful. Once, I forded one of these flooded rivers on horseback. With difficulty, I persuaded my mount to plunge into the water, then slipped over his croup and hung on to his tail, which I was able to use as a rudder. When I pushed it to the right the horse veered to the left and vice versa, and we eventually made a safe landing on the other side of the river. More usually, crossings were made in a *mar* boat, a tedious performance at the best of times. The *mar*, which was a ferry, consisted of a plank platform covering two open boats placed alongside one another. These were either paddled across the river or, connected by a running cable to another stretched across the river, were propelled from one side to the other by the force of the current.

This ingenious device worked very well, but constant adjustments had to be made to allow for the rise and fall of the rivers. A whole series of ghats, or landing places, had to be constructed at different levels on the river bank. Fortunately traffic was light and, although crossing took time, there were few delays. The other difficulty about travel anywhere in Assam during the rains was the fact that the dirt tracks soon became unusable by normal cars, and the Jeep had yet to be invented.

Once when touring with my family on the North Bank, we left our return rather late, or rather the monsoon broke rather early, and, although the roads were still motorable, driving became distinctly dicy. Most of the main roads were built on top of embankments to raise them well above the normal flood level, and they were narrow, single-track affairs. The road we were on became increasingly greasy, one skid led to another, and finally we slithered over the edge into a paddy field some six feet below the road. Paddy fields are divided into small enclosures by low banks in order to prevent the flood water running away, and we had one of the most bumpy rides of my experience before finding a way back onto the road.

At the start of our travels, before the rains broke, the roads had been so dry that the surface was almost invisible under a cloud of dust. Driving was difficult and one's destination uncertain. At one place, road work had been in progress, and one of the favourite hazards of road workers, a ramp, lay concealed from sight under the dust cloud. No warning signs were in use, or if they were they were not visible, nor was this one of the puny ramps usually encountered in civilised countries, but a step about six inches high. Needless to say, the impact when we hit it was considerable. As the car was carrying my wife, myself, the baby and her ayah, our servants and the usual mass of camp equipment, it says much for the motor engineers of those days that not a single spring was broken on either of these occasions. Probably the fact that we were packed like sardines in the car saved our bones.

The South Bank was more homely; distances were less and the terrain smaller. The reserve forests were mostly in one block. It was a country of low hills and valleys, the trees interspersed with villages and cultivation, and the forest itself, mostly of sal, had more the character of English woodland. Two comfortable forest bungalows served our needs. One at Kulsi was delightfully situated on a wooded spur above the river; the other, Rajapara, in a clearing, would have been equally charming if it had not been for the bats which lived in the roof. Their droppings were a constant reminder of their presence and the fusty smell of bat was ever with us. Larger, but less smelly, were the huge fruit-eating bats, with a wing span of five feet, which lived in a tree outside the bungalow and issued forth at dusk in search of food — a strange host of ghostly shapes gliding through the air on silent wings. Close to the bungalow was a large *bheel* where an earthquake had once lowered the surface, and the land became inundated with water. It was an eerie spot where tree skeletons still rose out of the water — a reminder that it had once been dry land.

In spite of its somewhat macabre associations, however, Rajapara was a pleasant place to work in, and the paddy fields where the jungle fowl gleaned the grain after harvest, and sometimes found their way into the pot, were cheerful, sunny and open spaces. But Kulsi was my favourite. The bungalow was surrounded by teak plantations, planted some sixty years before and now almost mature. In fact, growth in the Assam climate was too rapid to produce first-class teak and the local variety, though a useful furniture wood, was never up to Burma standards. Close by was a rubber plantation of *Ficus elastica,* but no tapping had taken place for some years, since Indian rubber was no longer able to compete with para rubber comercially. *Ficus elastica* belongs to the fig family, of which several species are found in Assam. Some grow to an immense size, having started life as climbing epiphytes on other trees. Eventually the host tree becomes completely encased by the *ficus* which forms a smooth bark around it — the host dies and the epiphyte takes over. Some, like the banian, send down aerial roots from their branches which help to buttress the huge bulk of the tree.

On the river bank was the *pilkhana,* the elephant depot, where our baggage animals were kept. The elephants frequently gave birth to babies, the progeny of wild bulls that had mated with the cows, and these were a constant source of entertainment. The calves' playground was a clearing dotted with tree stumps on which they balanced like circus elephants. They were friendly little beasts with endearing wrinkled faces and absurdly short trunks which they waved threateningly at us. The babies loved pitting their strength against ours and did their best to knock us over. The trouble was, that as they grew larger and stronger, they usually succeeded, and for this reason elephants born in captivity are often less tractable than those captured in the jungle which tend to have more respect for their masters.

From the bungalow we could watch the elephants being bathed in the river, while the gorials lay sunning themselves on the sandbanks and the calves had a whale of a time squirting one another with water. Instead of being pushed in prams, our babies went for elephant rides with their ayah.

Kulsi in those days was well known for its tigers, which were taken so much for granted by the locals that they treated them almost as domestic animals. I have seen a village woman throwing stones at a tiger that was lying too close to the path for her liking, and driving it away. We kept our ponies securely corralled near the bungalow at night, which was just as well because fresh tracks frequently appeared in the morning, evidence of a tiger who had visited the stable the night before.

The first rainy season, before our eldest daughter arrived on the scene, my wife, somewhat heroically in my opinion, accompanied me on a forest tour. We travelled round the forest bungalows, riding our ponies through the mud, constantly soaked by the rain and sweating it out in the heat. Such discomforts were forgotten in the cold weather when we were able to use our new car, a Ford V8 station wagon of which I was immensely proud. Wishing to impress my bride, I suggested a run in the forest on the first possible occasion. We set off one evening, only to be stopped by a puncture after passing the point of no return and reaching a place of some remoteness. It was then that I discovered that the spare wheel was firmly locked in place, that the ignition key did not fit the lock and that what I thought was simply a spare key had been left behind. It seemed we had a ten mile walk in front of us through the forest and through the night, something to which even the most intrepid and long-suffering of wives might justly have objected. It looked as though I was not to cut such an impressive figure after all, but I remembered that I had a rifle with me — a high velocity rifle and a powerful weapon. I had also been reading the works of Sapper in which the indomitable Bulldog Drummond shoots his way out of trouble, making light of locked doors. The trouble was that in this case the spare wheel lock was only about an inch from the petrol tank. I had a suspicion that if I missed the lock and hit the tank there would be a big bang and we would all go up in smoke. However, all was well; I took careful aim from what I hoped was a safe distance, scored a bull and shot the lock out of the centre of the wheel. My ego restored, we drove safely home.

Much of my work at this time consisted of marking trees for thinning, an interesting and engrossing task which is even more absorbing than golf. The idea was to select the best trees to be retained for the final crop and to remove those that were deformed, diseased or otherwise inferior, while preserving the correct spacing for the particular age of crop. Working at speed, this required a high degree of concentration.

I usually rode to and from my work, and Joy often came with me and met me again in the evening on her pony. There were pleasant rides along forest tracks, across the paddy fields and through orange orchards, where the oranges could be bought for the price of one rupee for as many as a villager could carry in a basket on his back. The village markets, where one could buy rice, vegetables, fish, fowls and fruit and, perhaps, some simple household utensils, were held once a week and were an invaluable source of supply.

When work was over for the day there was time to devote to the children or to take out my gun and look for something for the pot. At Christmas we usually spent the holiday at Kulsi, the bungalow decorated with red berries in lieu of holly and a large camp fire to sit by in the evenings. Of all the places I have known in Assam, it is of Kulsi that I have the happiest memories.

The rural economy was almost medieval. The ground was cultivated with wooden, ox-drawn ploughs that churned up the soil in the irrigated fields into a mud porridge. The land was divided into a series of scattered plots so that each villager got some of the best and some of the worst. The men tilled the soil, and later watched over the crops at night. When the crop was harvested, they carried home the sheaves slung on long poles borne on their shoulders. The women planted the rice seedlings in the mud and harvested the crop with sickles. When the sheaves reached the village they were winnowed outside on a spotlessly clean, sun-baked, mud floor. The children herded the cattle and, in the cold weather, the men collected firewood, hunted and fished. It was, on the whole, a pleasant life in which each member of the community had his or her part to play but not, as a rule, too arduous a one. When the harvest was safely in, there followed the harvest thanksgiving, the *Bihu*, with the lighting of bonfires and the drinking of much rice beer.

Each village community was more or less self-supporting, growing its own vegetables, catching its own fish and spinning and weaving its own cloth. The villagers also wove the silk spun by obliging worms. One silk worm ate the leaves of the mulberry and produced *muga,* a rather coarse, yellow silk which made excellent, long lasting sheets; another produced *endi,* a fine white silk, from the leaves of the castor oil plant. There were small hens which layed small, bantam-sized eggs and scratched a living round the primitive but scrupulously clean huts of the villagers; the cows produced little milk, but that didn't matter very much because it was considered unclean and undrinkable. The scavenging was done by the pigs. Fruit — mangoes, pineapples, bananas, oranges, papayas and coconuts, containing deliciously cool milk — grew in profusion. Cash crops included maize, ground-nuts, peppers, cotton, lentils and lac. Mustard, cultivated for its oil, embellished the greenery with vivid patches of yellow.

Each forest villager, in return for a low rent, was expected to give ten days' free labour to the department each year. But, as most of the villages had been in existence before the forests were reserved, this was always an unpopular demand, though not, in my opinion, an unreasonable one. As already hinted, the Assamese were not the world's most willing workers, and were not over-keen to work, even for money. Without the free labour system work in the forest would often have come to a standstill, or else outside labour would have had to be recruited which would have upset the village economy.

Each of the larger villages had its own school, dispensary and football pitch, where the teams played intrepidly with bare feet, and a number of villagers found their way to the university at Gauhati. Unfortunately, once a boy had become a BA, or even a failed BA, he usually considered it beneath his dignity to do any manual work, and more scholarly pursuits were hard to find. The goal of most graduates was government service of some kind.

In the Forest Department the higher posts were filled with members of the IFS, Europeans trained at British universities, and Indians from the forest college at Dehra. But, with the provincialisation of the service, the provincial forest service officers were being promoted to the higher ranks. A pile of applications adorned my desk from aspiring youths who sought such posts, or lesser ones as foresters or clerks, and it was my unpleasant task to turn most of them away for the simple reason that demand greatly surpassed supply.

The conservation and extraction of timber in the forest was as primitive as the agriculture, but largely for practical reasons. For one thing, there is no point in mechanisation when labour is both cheap and plentiful, nor did the forests usually lend themselves to mechanisation. Simul and other soft woods growing on or near the river banks could be, and were, made into rafts and floated to their destination, and a few plywood mills existed to deal with them. Logs from the giant, buttressed *Terminalia* species, reaching a height of 160 feet, were dealt with in this way. On the North Bank, in the Goalpara District, 45 miles of tramway had been built to extract timber from the sal forests, but, even here, maintenance proved expensive and, owing to road improvements, demand for its use was declining.

Except for a gregarious species like sal, the valuable trees were usually thin on the ground and often grew in inaccessible and hilly places, from which it would have been difficult to extract them to a central sawmill. Instead the logs were sawn *in situ* by sawyers, one of whom stood in the bottom of a pit while the others stood above, on a wooden platform on which the log was also balanced. Most of the sawyers were Nepalies who were masters of their craft. When converted, the timber was carried in bullock carts to rail head or roadside where it was loaded into railway trucks or lorries.

Sal was the most important timber. When converted into railway sleepers, it could resist the attack of white ants for ten years. The same trees provided telegraph posts, bridge and building timber. Many of the evergreens, with exotic names like gunserai, amari and poma, produced furniture timbers of high quality. But timber was not our only produce. What were classed as minor forest products — cane, lac, bamboos, reeds, thatching grass, medicinal fruits and firewood among them, were also in great demand.

The Assam forest department came into existence in 1862. By 1947 the province had nearly 7,000 square miles of reserved forest (11.6 per cent of the total land area), intended to be maintained as such in perpetuity, and over 14,000 square miles of unclassed state forest, which was gradually being opened up for cultivation as the population increased. Of the reserved forest, 1,674 square miles were being improved under working plans, designed to ensure a sustained yield of timber for all time. The percentage of valuable trees was increased by planting and by assisted natural regeneration, which involved the weeding of natural seedlings and the gradual opening up of the canopy as they grew in size. Thinning of stands was, of course, normal practice. In the sal forest, both controlled burning and controlled grazing was practised in order to inhibit the growth of the thatching grass and allow the sal seedlings to establish themselves. Sometimes, salt was spread on the grass to encourage cattle to eat the coarse and rather unpalatable leaves. Forest fires were a constant worry during the hot weather preceding the rains, in all but the evergreen forest, and fire protection was of considerable importance. Unlike many forest departments and most government departments, we achieved a modest profit.

In spite of the ever present threat of malaria and, at times, considerable discomfort, life in the jungle was always interesting and varied. In the '30s we had the satisfaction of feeling that we were doing a useful job, and that all was well in what may not have been in all senses the best part of the world but was, nevertheless, a very pleasant one.

However, there was a cloud on the European horizon which was worrying some of us. Believing that war might be unavoidable, I had applied for and been given a reserve commission in the Indian army, and periodically did my training with a regular cavalry regiment. In view of the fact that a considerable amount of time and money had been spent on my army training, I expected to be called up at any moment, but the summons failed to arrive.

Soon after the outbreak of war, Joy and I journeyed to Meerut, where I was attached to Hodgeson's Horse, but only in a temporary capacity for further training. Meerut, in the United Provinces, was in the heart of India, and quite different country from Assam. Tall, bearded men tilled the black soil and grew thickets of sugar cane; it was a flat, treeless country with a different smell, where the houses were built of brick and stone, and, on a cold weather morning, a heady ebullient climate that effervesced like dry champagne. We were still in India but might almost have been in a different land. As the regiment was in the course of being mechanised, and I was still in the horsed category, there was little of value that I could do. I once drove an antiquated tank and learnt something of its innards by numbers, but most of my time was spent exercising the regimental horses that were about to fade out of the picture. An enjoyable, but I couldn't help feeling, somewhat unprofitable exercise.

Then we returned to Assam, having visited, on our travels, the sad little cemetery at Lucknow where so many of the garrison, including a number of their children, ended their days during the Mutiny.

For those of us in India, it was a phoney war in those early days and a frustrating experience; we felt so out of the picture and unable to help our folk at home. Somewhat later, the forest department was given the task of supplying sawn hutting timber for the armed forces in the Middle East but, by and large, life in Assam went on much as usual. The Civil surgeons were army personnel seconded to the civil service, who were liable to be recalled to the colours in wartime. Our civil surgeon's orderly was reported to have been seen sharpening his master's sword on the veranda, but master was only called up much later, just in time to be caught in the net at Singapore. The two battalions of the 7th Gurkha rifles stationed in Shillong, and commanded by my brother-in-law, were being mechanised and learning to ride about in lorries instead of marching on their feet. There is a story, probably true, of one contingent of Gurkhas who were being trained to jump from the air. When told the height they would be flying one rifleman remarked naively that it was a long way to drop. He didn't seem to be particularly worried but was interested to hear that parachutes were to be provided.

We visited Shillong from time to time and there, too, life went on much as before. The Shillong races were as popular as ever, both among the Khasies and the Europeans. The Khasi jockeys rode tats, small ponies which they pulled unashamedly if it wasn't their turn to win — if all else failed, they fell off. Our ayah was a great punter who invariably spotted the winners or, we suspected, had been told beforehand which pony would come in first. As she said, "What would be the point of backing a loser?" We spent our holidays picnicking, bathing, playing tennis and golf and dancing at the club as we always had done, and nothing seemed likely to change in the foreseeable future. The dances at Government House, opened by the Governor and his lady leading the dignified State Lancers, no longer took place, but the Governor still wore his top hat at the races and mess dress was still worn in the officers' mess on guest nights.

In Europe the war dragged on — Norway, Dunkirk, the Battle of Britain. We listened to the wireless, felt guilty about living as we were, in comparative luxury, and wished we could play a more active role. But the military had agreed with the civil government not to call up or accept for military service anybody in a reserved occupation, and as all government servants were, there was nothing to be done about it.

Then in December 1941, the impossible happened; the American fleet was sunk at Pearl Harbour and within two months the invincible fortress of Singapore had fallen. In March many of our friends in the 7th Gurkha Rifles including my brother-in-law, had been killed in the four day battle at Bilin River, prelude to the fall of Rangoon. General Hutton's two divisions, virtually without air support, were inevitably in retreat before 70,000 crack Japanese troops. During the next two months the names of Burmese towns, each a little nearer to Assam, were announced over the air one by one as they fell to the enemy — Prome, Mandalay, Akyab, Mytkyina. The Chindwin was crossed at Kalowa and by 20th May, 12,000 ragged, starving and fever-ridden men, had climbed wearily up the hill paths into the state of Manipur on the Indian frontier and ended their 900 mile retreat.

There was little to stop the Japanese advance. The only possible fighting force left in Assam was a battalion of military police; the air defence of India depended on eight old Mohawk planes at Calcutta. In Assam there were neither landing strips nor anti-aircraft guns, and the only means of communication with the outside world were the paddle steamers of the Brahmaputra and a single track railway.

At last it seemed we were to be involved, with a vengeance. At any moment we expected to learn that the Japanese had reached Imphal, and to hear the drone of their bombers overhead. Mercifully, the enemy's communications had been stretched to the limit, and their forward troops were in no position to advance further. The men of 17 Div, who had reached Imphal in such a pitiable condition, had to remain to guard the frontier as there was no one to replace them, but there was no further advance by the Japanese before the monsoon rang down the curtain on the first act of the drama.

In the meantime, affairs in Assam were chaotic. In order to promote the interests of the local people European government servants were ordered to remain at their posts if Assam was occupied by the enemy. An order which, as far as I know, was never rescinded, in spite of the fact that in Burma everyone who obeyed it had been rounded up and placed behind wire. We hoped and prayed that these orders would not have to be obeyed.

Some 400,000 refugees had reached the province — Indians, Europeans, Burmese, men, women and children, all in a pitiable condition. Many more died on the way of cholera, dysentary or malaria. The civil and mission hospitals in Assam were filled with sick and wounded civilians and soldiers. Many lay on the floor for lack of beds. The troops on the border were eventually relieved, travelled down the slippery, narrow hill road and entrained at Manipur Road Station. It was left to the voluntary services to collect whatever they could lay their hands on, to brew soup, make tea and give the soldiers something to eat and drink as the trains halted at wayside stations.

Somebody at Army Headquarters in New Delhi noted on his map that the paths in the Naga Hills were called camel tracks and despatched a camel-borne medical unit to the new theatre of war. The wretched camels slipped and slithered in the sticky monsoon mud, broke their legs and their hearts and either died or had to be put out of their misery. The Indian Tea Association, with a more practical turn of mind, recruited a corps of tea garden managers and assistants who, with the help of the garden coolies, built camps along the refugee routes, organised supplies, and later started the road improvements so patently necessary.

Politically, the situation was worrying. Chandra Bose, an extreme nationalist, had visited Germany and Japan, and had recruited prisoners-of-war into an Indian National Army, which would join forces with the Japanese. Spies were seen under every bed, bridges were expected to be blown by saboteurs and a mass exodus of frightened Assamese to take place. But in India, open rebellion had been crushed by Wavell, and in Assam nothing explosive took place.

Although the immediate danger had passed the atmosphere was still electric; the smell of war was in the air and, however peaceful one's nature, the mood was catching. We were thankful that our families were safe, but, for the young, it was difficult to settle down once more to a normal, placid, peacetime life.

Soon I was to be transferred to Jorhat, which was to become the centre of military activity in the immediate future.

CHAPTER 7

War

WHEN WE ARRIVED Jorhat still had its peacetime appearance; the bungalow overlooked the *maidan*, a large, open, grassy space, and the war still seemed far away. While at Gauhati I had been offered a staff captaincy in the Timber Directorate, which had the task of organising timber supplies in India for the forces. I had turned it down because office work has never been my forte, and there seemed to be little point in putting on a uniform merely to warm a staff chair in New Delhi. The war was moving in our direction and I felt I should be doing a more useful job at the supply end. But when we arrived at Jorhat everything seemed so peaceful that I wondered if I had been mistaken.

The Jorhat bungalow was more sensibly designed that our Gauhati one — for one thing, my office was underneath while our living quarters were on top. It had a wide, shady, upstairs veranda and a pleasant compound. In some ways it was primitive, and our water came from a public tap in the road, usually with a long queue of resignedly patient water-carriers in attendance. Jorhat was now, however, the headquarters of Fourth Corps and soon the peaceful atmosphere was to become disrupted. A large base hospital was to spring up on the *maidan* with an evil-smelling incinerator. The smell was so appalling that we strongly suspected that the incinerator was being used for the disposal of corpses.

Eventually, we supplied much of the material for two hospitals, some five air strips, numerous bridges, a large REME workshop, a number of staging camps, and the great base which grew out of the jungle at Dimapur where the troops detrained at Manipur Road Station and embarked on their always-hazardous journey up the narrow, winding hill road to Kohima and Manipur.

The main air strip was at Jorhat, from which the Americans flew their Dakotas over the Hump, the 23,000 foot mountain ridge which separates Assam from China. The three hundred planes, which flew round the clock, were unarmed and were sometimes shot down by Japanese fighters. Others ran into thick fog and hit the mountain, but a steady stream of supplies got through, most of which reached Chiang Kai-Chek, for whom they were intended. The target was 20,000 tons a month, and the planes took off at three minute intervals. Our bungalow was in the direct line of flight, and the

Dakotas were so heavily loaded that by the time they reached us they barely cleared the roof of our bungalow. The noise of each flight was deafening, and for months our youngest daughter Jeannie, was kept awake at night and, when she did drop off, suffered from nightmares. Later, when we had returned home on leave and were staying with friends, she was still a bad sleeper. She used to wake up howling every evening and when we went up to comfort her would point at the dressing table and scream. All we could see was a plaster bust of Winston Churchill. The great man looked typically belligerent but that did not seem enough to account for our daughter's fears. Eventually we discovered that his face was luminous and shone with an eerie glow in the dark. When we switched on the light the luminosity, of course, disappeared.

Except for the marines the Americans were tough but sloppy, and extremely casual. We used to take the children in the car to the air strip to see the planes, and even drove along the runway without being challenged. Once, fighter planes suddenly shot out of a clump of bamboos and raced past us down the runway. We were still expecting the Japanese bombers and were advised to build a shelter in our compound, which we did, but we were to use it only once. In response to an air raid warning, which subsequently proved to be a false alarm, we collected the children and the servants and trailed through the wet grass in the dark. When we got to the shelter, we discovered a large and angry cobra already in occupation. After that we decided bed was the safest place.

There must be millions of snakes in India but one rarely sees them, and no one known to me was ever bitten. We had another encounter with a snake at Jorhat. It fell through the rotten ceiling cloth on to the table one evening as we were playing bridge, but dummy broke its back with a poker before any damage had been done. Once I was walking along a forest road, my head high in the air, watching some monkeys in the tree tops, when looking down I discovered I had just stepped over a banded krait, a beautiful, but deadly species, adorned with brilliant bands of yellow and black. If I had stepped on the reptile instead of over it, I would probably not be writing this today. On another occasion I entered the veranda of an inspection bungalow one evening and walked across the floor to the table. The lamp dimly illuminated what I took to be a walking stick leaning against, and protruding above, the table top. Wondering whose it could be, I stretched out my hand and was just about to take hold of the crook, when it came to life and drew back. The crook was, in fact, the coiled neck of a snake sitting on my chair, and it was about to strike. I took a leap backwards, which must have been a record long-jump in reverse, seized hold of a real stick and dispatched the intruder, a green reptile about six feet long.

There must, I suppose, have been others but these are the only three poisonous snakes that, to my knowledge, endangered my life while I was in India. In fact, I have seen more adders in the British Isles. My wife found another snake once, in the hole when she was about to pick up her ball on the eighteenth green at Shillong but fortunately spotted it in time. As for snake charmers, they never seemed to come our way.

We did sometimes come across the non-poisonous pythons which, I suppose, reach some thirty feet in length, but I have never heard of one attacking a human being in India. They, of course, crush their prey, breaking their bones before swallowing them, hence the name boa-constrictor. I believe that to do so, a python must have his tail anchored to a tree or some firm object. They can swallow incredibly large animals, and one I shot made up into extremely decorative handbags for my girl friends — only the skin of the under-surface is suitable. Pythons are, incidentally, very sound sleepers and are vulnerable when asleep.

The most likely time to find snakes, and the most dangerous, is when, for instance, turning over a pile of sticks or feeling for something in the undergrowth — just the sort of things that children like doing; otherwise snakes, like most wild creatures, usually do their best to get out of one's way. An exception in India is the King Cobra, which is the only aggressive Indian species that will attack unprovoked. Fortunately he was not a common snake in Assam.

With the arrival of the army and air force, life in Assam became very different from what it had been before. The bucolic peace had been shattered, the tempo of life had increased, and strange faces and figures clad in jungle green were visible everywhere. Punjabi, Sikh and British troops, gum-chewing American GIs, and broadly smiling East Africans roamed the streets of Jorhat; the planters' club became more of an officers' mess and Americans sprawled in the wicker chairs in a manner which formerly would have brought down the wrath of the memsahibs on their heads. Sometimes we had a film evening and once, a girl in a travel-stained white dress, called Vera Lynn, sang to us nostalgically about the white cliffs of Dover.

As the pressure against the Japanese built up and men returned from the front for a brief spell of leave, the consumption of alcohol increased, and so did the number of jeeps that ran amok. When I went on tour and had to leave the family behind, I accepted a police guard to protect them, not from the Assamese but from a possibly drunk and licentious soldiery. The snoring of the guard did little to dispel my wife's fears, but may possibly have scared off any potential intruders.

Now that the army was occupying Jorhat in force, servants were hard to come by; they naturally tended to infiltrate the American lines where the wages were highest. Our *pani* walla asked for leave one day and, when asked why, replied that he wished to draw his pay at the American base. As he had been working regularly for us this was rather surprising, but not as surprising as his ingenuous explanation. Apparently he had signed on with the USAF Transport Command but his only contact with his new employers was on pay day. Deeply impressed by such initiative, we granted him leave.

Another member of our staff, one of my official orderlies, was an Ahom with a deformed foot which was to be his undoing. One day, our store room was broken open and some stores were found to be missing. In the dust of the floor was my orderly's unmistakable footprint, and he confessed his guilt. I had never liked the man and this was an excellent opportunity to get rid of him. Probably for this reason I let him off with a fine. Although he deserved to get the sack I couldn't help feeling that I was prejudiced. On the whole our servants, although maddening at times, worked for us and stuck to us loyally during those difficult days.

These were strange days indeed for those of us who were used to the solitude of the jungle and the small world of rural India. Some of our tea planter friends had joined V Force, a hush-hush organisation which, with the help of Naga scouts, patrolled the forward areas and kept an eye on the Japanese advance troops. Sometimes minute planes landed on the polo ground at Jorhat with wounded from the front line and, occasionally, a few Japanese prisoners would be brought in. It was a point of honour with the Japanese, though, to die fighting. Those that were captured usually tried to commit suicide.

The Jorhat shops soon ran out of European stores and, because of the army's requirements, prices of local produce soared. Whisky, almost a must with many Europeans as a pick-me-up in the debilitating monsoon climate, was practically unobtainable, and spirit drinkers had to make do with Indian rum. There was an enterprising, but somewhat naive, Indian who wished to start a still, and made enquiries to find out where he could procure whisky essence. Some crates of whisky occasionally got through from somewhere for the civilians. A planters' club once got hold of some bottles of Scotch, or so they thought. It proved to be a particularly fiery and undrinkable brand of fiery liquor. Some genius had bored holes through the bottle, extracted the whisky and substituted his own noxious brew. The army did better, getting its whisky in bulk. On one occasion a railway waggon, carrying the precious cargo, was derailed. The Americans stationed a guard over it — the British supplied another guard to keep an eye on the Americans.

Pilfering was rife, and one thief got away unknowingly with a truckload of corpses on their way to the burial ground. An Indian engine driver forced open a crate containing hand grenades. He took one of these strange things back to his cab, decided it was no use to him and threw it into the furnace, with disastrous results.

We had a constant stream of visitors, mostly officers and other ranks on short leave, and, at night, the veranda of our bungalow was often strewn with slumbering bodies. My wife rented a cottage in Shillong and took the children there during the rains, while I took in a mixed bag of PGs. The most exalted was a REME colonel, whose rations were a godsend and, at the other end of the scale were two pacifist members of the Friends Ambulance Unit who wore an army-type uniform and were worried because they were constantly being saluted.

I would sometimes take a party of our army friends to see the game sanctuary, and spend a happy morning riding through the high grass on elephants watching the rhino, the water buffalo and the deer. As we set off through the early morning mist we were back in another world. As far as possible we tried to keep the wheels turning normally in the forest department, but most of our energies were directed towards supplying the vast quantities of forest produce so urgently needed by the armed forces. We spent time, too, trying to persuade ignorant supply officers not to make fools of themselves — an operation requiring both tact and firmness.

One such enthusiast indented for a large quantity of thatching grass, which he imagined would provide excellent fodder for his mules. It was with the utmost difficulty that he was dissuaded. Thatch is a coarse grass, only eaten by buffaloes which have tongues made of sand-paper. If the mules had been foolish enough to sample such fare, their tongues would have been badly blistered.

A member of the Burma Public Works Department, who had been drafted into the army as a sapper, was unable to persuade a staff officer that, because a road was shown as metalled on the map of Burma this was not necessarily the case — in spite of the fact that the sapper had himself built the road. Fortunately the Forest Department retained its civilian status and, not being in uniform, we were able to stand up to the brass hats when they had some particularly hare-brained scheme that was relevant to forestry.

While stationed at Jorhat, our second daughter was born in Shillong, bringing our total offspring at the time to three — two girls and a boy. The boy, William, at the age of five, drove a guest's jeep across the compound and attempted to enter my office. My own transport was a 15 cwt army truck of a type discarded by the army because the wheels kept shearing off. Fortunately we discovered that they had been incorrectly put on and the fault was remedied. Equally fortunately, the controls were out of the reach of my enterprising son.

The new baby girl was born just after an earthquake had shaken us up. It rocked our Jorhat bungalow, shook all the plaster off the walls and sent the pictures and ornaments crashing to the ground, surprisingly breaking only one of them. Fumes rose from ominous cracks in the ground, and the one and only brick building in the town came crashing down like a house of cards. The same earthquake had been felt, but not so violently, in Shillong, while my wife was at the club and a dance was in progress. After a pause, the band struck up God Save the King and, morale restored, the dance continued. When I wrote to Joy and suggested that she postpone her return, she thought I was exaggerating the state of chaos, and arrived to be sadly disillusioned. For weeks the children enjoyed themselves, falling into buckets of whitewash and heaps of wet plaster as the PWD hastened slowly to straighten things out.

A large part of my time was spent at the Manipur Road base, co-ordinating supplies with the engineers. At Jorhat the shops might be empty, but there was an army store at Dimapur, for which I had a pass, where one could buy things like sardines and even sweets, which the children hadn't seen for months. The snag was that I usually wore a khaki shirt and shorts and had never been very dressy. Probably I looked as though I had just walked out of Burma, and was sometimes picked up as a deserter. As I had usually left my identity card behind this sometimes led to a certain amount of inconvenience. At other times I would forget the pass word when challenged on the way back to my camp after a few drinks in the engineers' mess *basha.* To be suddenly confronted by a line of fixed bayonets is disconcerting. Soon the Manipur Road base was to grow into a small town and, where before there had been nothing but bamboos and undergrowth and the chattering of monkeys, there appeared acres of huts, concrete roads and a cinema. The forest department had installed a saw mill to expedite the supply of timber, and the army had its own mobile forest unit.

Once or twice I followed the greatly improved road to Kohima and Manipur, to chase up timber supplies in the hills and have a look at the forward areas. The road was never very reliable because it had originally been built on the wrong side of the valley. In other words, the dip of the strata ran the wrong way and, during the rains, landslides were frequent.

Considering that everything and everyone travelling by rail had to journey for 800 miles by narrow gauge tracks from the main line at Parbatipur and be shipped across the Brahmaputra, it was something of a miracle that the troops and supplies needed for the invasion of Burma ever materialised. Once when I went to the Manipur Road station to meet the Calcutta train, I was surprised and overjoyed to find it apparently almost on time. However, I was wrong. "Oh no, Sir, the train is not on time. It is yesterday's train that approaches so timely", the station master explained disarmingly.

One day, while in the CRE's office at Dimapur, attempting to satisfy his endless craving for bamboos, a staff sergeant entered the basha to inform his CO that he had shot an elephant. He had apparently been out with another NCO looking for something with four legs to shoot with their .303 army rifles. Seeing an elephant which seemed to be in difficulties in the river they had decided, so they said, to put it out of its misery. When I asked if the elephant was now dead they were quite indignant. They assured me that they had pumped over twenty rounds into it at short range and were not inconsiderable marksmen. They did not, of course, know that I was a forest officer or realise what a serious crime they had committed in the eyes of the civil authorities. As there was a war on, I decided to accept the shikaris' explanation and, collecting two of my forest guards, we set off along the river bank with the two soldiers to inspect the elephant.

The elephant lay motionless in the centre of a deep pool, apparently floating on the surface, and quite dead. The shikaris had, however, been using ammunition with the sharp noses of the bullets sawn off. I wasn't at all sure that even twenty soft nosed bullets would have reached a vital spot, and to make sure that it was dead, we threw stones at the animal. Much to the surprise of the two NCOs, but not to me, the elephant immediately came to life, struggled violently and then relapsed once more into a state of torpor or, more exactly, suspended animation.

What had happened, we decided, was that the elephant having apparently tried to swim the river while in flood, must have been washed downstream. Just below the surface of the water floated the broken branch of a tree, firmly anchored in some invisible manner to the bottom — it was probably attached to a sunken log. At the end of the branch was a fork into which the animal's head was firmly stuck; presumably it had floated into it and the force of the water had prevented its getting out again. It was impossible to find a vital part of the almost totally submerged elephant to shoot at, in order to deliver the *coup de grace*, and the problem was to know what to do with it.

Eventually I decided to attempt to capture the elephant alive, but this wasn't going to be easy because there were no *koonkies* in the district.

However, I sent one of the guards back for a rope, while the other guard and I stripped and swam round the pinioned animal. When the rope arrived, we were joined by the third man and commenced a somewhat bizarre operation — as far as I know the first and only case of an elephant being landed on the end of a line.

While one of the forest guards stayed in the water I climbed onto its back with the other one, fervently hoping that the *hathi* was as firmly stuck as it seemed to be. Never having had two humans on its back before, the animal was naturally indignant. It writhed and wriggled while we slipped and slithered on the wet surface of its body enjoying, if that is the right word, the same sensations that used to delight the young at country fairs when they attempted to cross the 'cake walk'. But the cake walk was child's play compared to this elephant ride; for one thing, the fair people hadn't thought of including an elephant's trunk in their entertainment. Somehow we managed to avoid the flailing proboscis and succeeded in hobbling the elephant's kicking legs.

The final act in the drama was the cutting of the branch to free the elephant. While the end of the rope was firmly held on the bank, one of the guards hacked at the branch with his *dao* and, as it fell apart, dived hastily into the water and swam rapidly ashore. The elephant had put up such a fight that we wondered what would happen when it was freed, but it must have worn itself out because it just floated gently downstream before finding its feet. By slow degrees and frequent tugs on the rope we coaxed our catch up a shelving beach onto dry land and secured it firmly to a tree.

The elephant was weak, but its wounds appeared to be superficial. I was too busy to devote more time to the invalid but ordered the local forester to send for a *koonkidar* and the nearest vet and, in the meantime to see that adequate food and water was provided. I departed, feeling confident that the animal would recover; but this was not to be. Once out of the water, the wounds suppurated and the elephant died before veterinary treatment could be applied. We had done all we could for the unfortunate beast but there is no knowing for how long it had been trapped in the river, and a score or more bullets in its hide cannot have done it any good. Death was, perhaps, inevitable.

About this time I had another adventure with an elephant — on this occasion one of our departmental ones. From time to time we did have trouble with our domesticated bulls, particularly when in *musth,* the condition in elephants which corresponds with rut in deer, and is accompanied by the discharge of a dark fluid from the temporal glands. Our bull elephants sometimes attacked their attendants when not in *musth,* probably due to some provocation, real or imagined, by the animal. We had a fine departmental elephant, a tusker called Akbar, which killed three men. One may well ask why Akbar was given a second, let alone a third, chance. Such killings were, however, accepted as part of the natural order of things, one of the accepted hazards of looking after elephants. Akbar was normally the most docile of animals but, because he was known to have fits of bad temper, his attendants had been ordered to take special precautions. Instead of being wafted aloft on his trunk, the grass-cutter had been ordered to engage his attention from in front while the mahout climbed on his back from the tail end. He was provided with a second grass-cutter so that the same procedure could be followed when he went to collect his fodder for the night.

Unfortunately, after a time the men became careless, and preferred to take risks rather than adopt such an undignified method of mounting their charge. Akbar made his fatal lunge and ran one of the men through the stomach with one of his tusks. There was nothing we could do for him, and he died soon afterwards. The other two killings, at which I was not present, followed a similar course. Immediately afterwards Akbar was his normal self, and I don't believe he was in any way mad — just a bit quick-tempered and, unfortunately the possessor of a long pair of tusks.

The adventure to which I referred was not, however, with Akbar but with an elephant in an advanced stage of *musth* and in an obviously dangerous state. He was as big as Akbar but a *makhna* without tusks and was, at the time, at Jamuguri, where I had paid my first visit some years before to the Assam jungle. I arrived one evening at the inspection bungalow to find the village in a state of siege, and to be told that the *makhna* had broken his fetters, was at large and in an extremely black and ugly mood — would I please do something about it. Again, no *koonkies* were available.

The elephant was indeed making a nuisance of himself, breaking into the village rice stores, chasing any villager who came into his line of sight, uprooting plantain trees and indulging in an orgy of vandalism. The villagers stayed indoors, hoping that the *goonda* would not decide to break through the fragile walls of their houses, and the village school remained closed. Those who had to go abroad did so looking back over their shoulders. Elephants were valuable animals and, although it might be unavoidable, I decided it would hardly be politic to shoot the *makhna* without making an attempt at capture. One of the villagers, either a hero or a fool, volunteered to sit in a tree and jump on the elephant's back as it passed underneath. In fact, he insisted on sitting in the tree but unfortunately the *makhna* refused to come near it.

I was at my wit's end to know what to do and was on the point of shooting the vandal when an Anglo-Burman arrived at my camp. He was a refugee who had been a member of the Burma subordinate forest service and, having been re-employed by the Assam Government, had been told to report to me. I felt rather sorry for the lad, arriving at such an awkward and frightening time while the village was in a state of turmoil, but I need not have worried. He wasn't in the least perturbed and merely asked if we had any opium.

The sale of opium, which is eaten not smoked in Assam, was prohibited, except under licence to addicts. There were, however, a number of these, and a well-stocked black market for the benefit of the non-registered. Opium was rightly banned, but the drug is a stimulent as well as a narcotic and without it the jungle folk would have found it difficult to get through the rains. With the help of opium, a man can keep going for days under conditions that would kill most people, and the elephant mahouts were no exception. They were avid opium eaters and were useless without the drug. There was no difficulty in getting hold of some for the elephant.

A piece about the size of a golf ball was given a coating of molasses. We waited until the delinquent was on a path with a clean, smooth surface, and then one of us approached as near as he dared, and rolled the ball towards the elephant. We held our breath while the rogue smelt the strange object and at last picked it up and put it in his mouth. Soon a happy smile replaced the look of defiance on the elephant's face and we cautiously moved in his direction. With a little persuasion, he took a somewhat unsteady trip to the elephant lines and, when he came to his senses, was firmly shackled to a tree. Our troubles were over.

In the meantime, preparations for the reoccupation of Burma had been continuing. Some 250,000 tea garden coolies had been improving the road from Dimapur to Imphal and beyond to Tamu. Six thousand tons of supplies were arriving daily by rail at Dimapur and the Ledo base in upper Assam. The Ledo road, leading eventually to China and employing another 70,000 coolies, was started in 1942 and completed within two years at a cost of $137,000,000, and with a final length of 1,040 miles from Ledo to Kumnming. Wingate's Chindits were busy behind the Japanese lines in Burma. The wounded and sick from these raids, suffering from malaria, jaundice, typhus, dysentary, Naga sores and wounds were, if lucky, evacuated by two flying boats, Gert and Daisy.

On March 7th, 1944, the Japanese launched a massive offensive with 100,000 crack Imperial troops. We didn't realise what was happening at the time; we only knew that Tiddim had been evacuated by 17 Div and that 20 Div had withdrawn from Tamu. One day in March I was motoring back to

Jorhat, at the end of a tour of inspection, when I met a cloud of dust which stretched apparently unendingly down the dirt road. Under cover of the dust was a long convoy of army lorries. When I realised that they were travelling in the wrong direction, that is away from the war zone, my enquiries elicited the information that the lorries contained Admin. personnel and stores from Dimapur — the Japanese were closing in on Manipur and Kohima, and a large scale battle was imminent.

Feeling rather lonely, I continued my journey in the opposite direction. The news was distinctly worrying because a successful push by the Japanese into the plains would have cut off Jorhat and upper Assam from the rest of India. No doubt our families would have been evacuated by air, but a Japanese success of this magnitude would have seriously upset the allied plans and endangered the rest of India. As we were to learn later, the immediate Japanese objective had been to cut the railway, overrun the airfields and put a stop to the air traffic over the Hump to China.

I thought I had better pay my staff at Dimapur a visit and boost their morale. In fact, they were wonderful — not a man absconded, although Japanese patrols were reported to have been seen within five miles of the base. During April the siege of Kohima began and lasted for 16 days — 3,500 of the besieged against 15,000 Japanese. The garrison was a mixed one of Assam Rifles, contingents of the Burma Regiment, some Gurkhas, Mahrattas and Punjabis, and a miscellanea of sappers, pioneers, transport personnel, ambulance drivers and a medical unit. To add to their difficulties, there were 1,500 wounded in the Kohima hospital.

At one time, the Deputy Commissioner's compound was partly in enemy and partly in allied hands. The DC, Charles Pawsey, had wisely moved into the army lines. Water had to be fetched at night from a spring within thirty yards of the enemy position, and was rationed to one pint per man daily, Kohima, 5,000 feet up in the Naga Hills, had no air strip and supplies had to be dropped; the battle area was so small that many loads fell among the enemy.

The Imphal siege lasted for three months, during which 300 planes unloaded supplies each day and 30,000 wounded were evacuated by air. The Japanese claimed that Imphal had fallen on 30th March and Kohima on 4th April. Fortunately this was not so and the bridgehead to India was held.

Standing in the wings, as it were, I had the heartening experience of watching the relieving troops arrive at the Manipur Road Station. Tracks were laid between each pair of open trucks, and a ramp was let down at one end of the train. In a few minutes, the armoured vehicles were off, ready to make their way up the hill. The 6th Indian Division, a brigade of the 33rd

Indian Corps from Arakan, and the 4th Royal West Kents were flown to Dimapur and, at the Battle of Summerhouse Hill, the Siege of Kohima was finally raised by the Royal Berkshire Regiment.

Three days after the relief of Kohima, I thumbed a lift in a jeep up the Manipur Road. Practically nothing was left of Kohima — the once-cheerful hill station had been rased to the ground. What had been a village was a sea of mud with a few blasted trees still standing like ghostly sentinels, and with the stench of death in the air. War is not a pretty thing.

Five miles further up the road our guns were firing, but it was not until 22nd June that the advancing troops joined up with those of Fourth Corps eight miles from Imphal. It was not until December that the Imphal plain was clear of Japanese. In March of the following year Rangoon was reoccupied and two months later Germany surrendered unconditionally to the Allies.

Life in Assam slowly returned to normal; the jungle began to encroach on the now silent and deserted air strips and the camps stood empty and forlorn. The carcasses of abandoned vehicles began to sink into the jungle like drowning men. The Superintendent of Police at Jorhat took to collecting abandoned jeeps as a hobby and, at one time, had six parked under his bungalow.

In 1945, having spent eight years without a break in India, my family and I were granted four months' compassionate leave in the United Kingdom. The day before we were due to leave Jorhat, we learnt that there was cholera in Bombay and that we must all be inoculated. Early in the morning of the day of our departure we paid a visit to the local dispensary and persuaded a sleepy doctor babu to give us our jabs.

The police department at Jorhat owned a sinister black van which had served as a hearse as well as a Black Maria. The kindly Superintendent of Police had offered us the use of this vehicle to get to Gauhati. As the railway was still in a state of chaos, and as I no longer owned a car and had perforce to leave my 15 cwt truck with my successor, we had gladly accepted this offer. We set off full of hope, but the Black Maria was in a black mood that day. After a few miles we had to deal with a blocked petrol pipe, and three stops further on the fan belt broke. We reached Gauhati in a cloud of steam, staggered on to Pandu and arrived just after our train had left. We slept in a stationary railway coach with neither lights nor fans, and twenty-four hours later got under way. We just reached Bombay in time to board a troop ship before she sailed.

There was said to be a Japanese submarine at large in the Indian Ocean and the blackout, and the necessity for keeping the porthole of our cabin closed in a ship not designed for the tropics, was something of an ordeal. We were not in convoy, and kept our fingers crossed. The daily boat drills with three small children were sheer hell but the food, after our spartan diet of the last few months, was marvellous. I remember I got hooked on fried tripe.

We landed safely at Southampton, where Joy and I and the three children eventually found a vacant hotel room, with one double bed into which we all squeezed for the night. Southampton was pock-marked with bomb damage; England was veiled in fog. The people seemed strained and preoccupied, and their pale skins looked ugly and unhealthy after the smiling, brown faces of the East. We were glad to be home, but felt like strangers in a strange land.

In August, with a sense of shock, we heard of Hiroshima and Nagasaki, the final spine-shivering act of an horrific war. Whether the 'bomb' resulted in less human misery than a prolonged campaign would have caused, is arguable. What is not, is that this was the introduction of a new dimension of horror in warfare, and its memory is not easy to live with. It has been suggested that the Japanese knew they were beaten in May, before the bomb was dropped, but that Truman was unaware of that fact.

CHAPTER 8

Journey's End

FOR ME the four months' leave came to an end all too soon. Joy and our family were unable to get a passage to India, and I had to return alone. I sailed from Liverpool on a cold winter's day in a comfortable ship, a carefree member of a stag party of returning officials, and in due course arrived back in Assam. Soon afterwards, I was elevated to the rank of Junior Conservator, in charge of the Assam Valley, and found myself in possession of Forest Lodge. The bungalow was by rights the official residence of the Senior Conservator but, fortunately for me, he was an Indian with his own house in Shillong. The house was built on a pleasant site on high ground, surrounded by trim lawns, and with a red, tin roof, was somewhat fantastically designed. With its turrets and cones, it had something of the air of a French Chateau or a Scottish Mansion with, perhaps, just a touch of the Burmese pagoda — Swiss Gothic is, I believe, the current description.

My first task was the Herculean one of unravelling and picking up the threads that had become entangled during the war, and helping to get the department back on an even keel. Our chief bugbear was the audit, and the least welcome part of the exercise was the straightening out of the accounts. Early in the war, a unit requiring forest produce had indented on the Timber Directorate through its normal channels, and the request had been passed on to us in the tortuous manner beloved of bureaucrats and auditors. But when Assam became an active service area, and the Japanese were at our front door, the normal regulations had been considerably bent. During the emergency our depot keepers had been authorised, in fact ordered, to supply forest produce without delay to anyone who asked for it and could produce an authoritative chit. By agreement with the army top brass, such chits were to be honoured by the War Department when presented for payment. Unfortunately, however, our none-too-literate or knowledgeable depot keepers had not always been capable of deciding what bore the stamp of authority and what did not. As the forest revenue, by the last year of the war, increased by more than £600,000 or 600 per cent over the normal prewar annual figure, this was a serious matter.

The motto of the 14th Army was 'God help those who help themselves', and some of the signatories of the chits had been men of imagination. Now that the accounts were being settled, those who had to foot the bill were, perhaps understandably, reluctant to honour chits apparently signed by Adolf Hitler, Rommel, Lord Haw-Haw and Charlie Chaplin. How I longed for a herd of goats to devour all this unwelcome correspondence! But in time things sorted themselves out and we slowly got back to doing them in a way which the auditors could understand.

We were offered a free gift of surplus American equipment, and I had to choose from a long list what I thought might be of use to the department. Having personally answered an advertisement and acquired a pair of wide-fitting army surplus boots, I was rather wary of being caught once again — the boots were indeed wide-fitting, having apparently been intended for the East African Regiment, and for feet the size of snowshoes. However, I finally chose a number of outboard motors, electrical generating plants, some portable sawmills, together with a bulldozer and a high-powered pair of field glasses. All of which proved to be of some use, except the bulldozer which was a bit too sophisticated for us.

The biggest headache was probably brought on by the five year plan which involved columns of figures and, as the future was so uncertain and computers were not a part of our equipment, a good deal of faith. There had been little recent investment in forest buildings, and silvicultural operations had been minimised during the war, so the plan eventually gave the forest department a much-needed shot in the arm. We were even able to build our own foresters' training college.

The forest department was under the charge of the forest minister, a member of the Assam Legislative Assembly and, when my Indian superior retired and I sat in the chair of the Senior Conservator, I became involved at first hand with politics. The minister was a decent chap, who genuinely had the welfare of the forests at heart, and who did his best to understand our problems. But he also had a host of cousin-brothers, most of whom seemed to be seeking employment or contracts in and with his department, and constituents who wanted to cultivate land in the forests reserves. There were also the members of my own staff who had the minister's ear, and who either objected to their postings or believed their promotion to be unduly slow. To do the minister justice, he was not unreasonable in view of all these commitments, and interfered only occasionally in the running of the department. He had the advantage of being somewhat better used than I to the affairs of state, but I was better informed about the forests. Our discussions took up a lot of time but, on the whole, we got on well together. It was nice to be at the top but I missed those former carefree days in the *mofussil,* and how I loathed the bureaucratic machine. We were responsible for inflicting bureaucracy on India but the Indians have made the whole thing into a fine art.

Eventually my family received their sailing orders and we were united once more, but their passage to India was not a particularly happy one. The children had just recovered from chicken-pox when they left England, and had scarcely embarked when they developed whooping cough. At least, that was what Joy and most of the passengers called it, including a woman who shared their cabin at the start of the voyage but thereafter beat a hasty retreat. The ship's doctor, however, uninfluenced by the children's whooping and retching and determined not to have any such infectious disease on his ship, adamantly refused to acknowledge the whoops. My wife spent her time feeding and tending the children in their cabin in which they were incarcerated, and being treated like a leper by her fellow passengers. To add to her difficulties, when she left to snatch a hasty meal in the saloon, our youngest daughter, objecting to the incarceration, insisted on exploring the bowels of the ship, hotly persued by her elder sister. As she was barely three and Jackie was only six, this must all have been rather worrying for my over-burdened wife.

In the meantime, I had set out to meet the ship at Bombay, where political agitators had been active and the windows of European shops were being smashed. I decided to leave the children's ayah, who had accompanied me so far, at Calcutta, as it seemed unreasonable to subject her, unnecessarily, to any possible danger, and completed the journey on my own.

I was being well-paid, but I am one of those people whose money seems to evaporate in a mysterious manner. As I had to meet the expense of the journey to and from Bombay out of my own pocket, and as by first class this was a not inconsiderable sum, I decided to make the outward journey by inter class. This was a form of transport intermediate in comfort or discomfort, whichever way you looked at it, between the luxury of the first class and the extreme austerity of the third. The seats, though harder than those of the first and second class compartments, were thinly padded and the compartments, patronised by the babu class and the less affluent Europeans were normally not too full. But when I arrived on the platform at Calcutta, I discovered that the third class coaches were full and the third class passengers had overflowed into the inter compartments. The train was about to pull out of the station and, having no alternative, I hastily joined them.

The compartment, like all the rest, was full to capacity and bursting at the seams. The upper bunks, which were meant for sleepers, were fully occupied by sitters, and I wedged myself into a small space on one of them between a woman who was nursing a baby at her breast and another nursing a baby goat on her knee. There was one babu in the compartment wearing a clean white dhoti but the rest of my fellow passengers were peasants of all creeds and castes, one or two sepoys returning from leave, an off-duty police constable and an assortment of children of varying ages.

Considering that communal riots were bedevilling India at the time, the different creeds were getting on famously, as they mostly do when not egged on by agitators, but I was a bit worried as to what kind of reception I should get. Although I had spent most of my life in India with the jungle folk, I had always been in a position of authority. Now I was just one of the crowd in a packed railway compartment, taking up some of the much-needed space. India was also, at this time, in a state of tension waiting for the curtain to lift while the politicians argued with one another, and the British tried to preserve a united India. The riots in Bombay were a symptom of frustration and I wondered how I should be received in this microcosm of the Indian scene.

I need not have worried. The Indian people are among the friendliest and best-mannered in the world and, unless maddened by mob hysteria, vent their spleen on the system and the Government and not on the individual. My fellow travellers couldn't have been more friendly and, apart from the discomfort, the thirty-six hour journey across India was one of the pleasantest I have made. I was offered oranges and bananas, my cigarettes were accepted and smoked in return, and I was made to feel thoroughly at home. At Bombay, I discovered that the riots were over and, having been united with my family, we had a more uneventful and conventional journey back to Assam.

Shillong is a delightful place with a reasonable climate, where pine trees and rhododendrons are at home, and English flowers and vegetables grow happily in the gardens. It was a good spot in which to have one's headquarters.

The Khasi Hills were a part of the administrative area known as the Khasi and Jaintia Hills District, the latter being the hill country between the Khasi and North Cachar Hills. The people of both are similar, being a mongoloid race who, like the Nagas, probably entered Assam from the south east. The Khasia and Jaintias, however, have been subject to different influences and came under British rule in different ways. In the case of the Khasi Hills, the take-over was almost entirely peaceful, resulting from a series of treaties with the several native clan chieftains, the Siems, which left them considerable independence. Shillong was never, in fact, a part of British India, but was leased from the Siem of Mylliem.

The Jaintia people were ruled by a single raja, and the British take-over in 1835 was primarily due to what the Jaintias considered an unreasonable

dislike of human sacrifice on the part of the British, who objected to the
kidnapping of Indians from the Nowgong district to be offered up to the local
goddess. Whereas the Khasis were, and many still are, simple animists, the
Jaintias have been considerably influenced by Hinduism and its taboos, such
as those affecting the eating of beef and the drinking of milk.

The first British presence in the Khasi Hills was at Cherrapunjee where,
in 1830, a sanatorium was established for convalescent soldiers from Calcutta
— not an altogether happy choice, because the site chosen was the wettest
place in the world, where a record fall of 902 inches was recorded in 1861.
The deluge begins when the vapour-filled clouds of the monsoon strike the
high cliffs of the Cherrapunjee escarpments and, as most of the rain falls in
three months, from mid-June to mid-September, it can be a depressing spot
at that time of the year. In addition to a record rainfall, the sanitorium had a
record rate of suicides, for whose destruction the cliffs towering above the
plain below couldn't have been more suitably contrived. By the time the
monsoon reaches Shillong, which is under thirty miles away as the clouds
fly, its fury has abated considerably, and the mean annual rainfall is around
70 inches. It was here that a site was more wisely chosen when it was decided
to build a hill station — an altogether drier and more cheerful place.

Until the 1930s, the steep climb from the Surma Valley to Cherrapunjee
and on to Shillong had to be made along bridle paths, and the less energetic
visitors were carried up to the top of the escarpment on the backs of coolies.
In the old days, soldiers were not alone in seeking the cool air of the hills, and
many civilian families must have made the trek from the torrid plains to
Shillong where the children could get some colour in their cheeks. Along
one of these tracks is a sad and lonely tombstone which marks the last resting
place of 'a child called Camilla', who arrived too late and died within a few
miles of Shillong in 1843, one of the multitude of European children who
died in India at an early age.

But Shillong had a smiling face, as befitted a hill station to which people
usually came for a brief spell to recuperate and enjoy themselves. Far below
the 6,500 Shillong Peak, the white houses nestled among the pine trees. The
official bungalows and hotels had large gardens, and the red roads carried
little traffic. Most of the older bungalows had in their compounds what were
known as *bibighars* — smaller bungalows where the bachelor occupants of
the larger ones were wont to keep their Khasi mistresses, concealed from the
eyes, if not the knowledge of the memsahibs. In my day, these bungalows
were more often used as spare bedrooms.

With its golf course, polo, racing and club; the Government House Balls
and the mess nights when the Gurkha pipers piped round the room; with its

numerous private dinner parties, Shillong was a gay and lively place. For those who preferred their own company, or to have their girl friends to themselves, there were secluded picnic places, with or without bathing pools, and for those who loved horses as well as girls, charming rides through the pine woods, each named after a Governor's daughter.

Before the war, the Government House balls were stately affairs, where medals and decorations were worn and programmes provided, complete with pencils attached, for booking one's dances. An invitation to the Ball was a command, and an ADC was stationed at the entrance to Government House to make sure that we had all clocked in. However, once HE and his lady had opened the ball with the State Lancers, there was nothing to prevent the unsociable, and the indifferent dancers, from walking out again at the back.

Most governors provided a sumptuous buffet supper on these occasions but one, who was rather mean, deceived his guests by a cunning ruse. The table appeared to have its full complement of gorgeous creations but the best, like the doll's house confectionery stolen by Huncka Muncka and Tom Thumb in Beatrix Potter's immortal tale, were made of plaster. An ADC stood over them to prevent the guests breaking their teeth.

Once, when we had had our fill of high life, Joy and I packed a rucksack and trekked along the bridle paths into the interior of the district without any servants — an almost unheard of thing for a sahib to do — and camped each night at an inspection bungalow.

Among the residents of Shillong were some old characters who added interest to our daily lives. The Deputy Commissioner was a talented but absent-minded individual who was always parking his car and then forgetting where he had left it, an annoying habit but one which at least gave the local police something to do. Once, after driving his wife to Gauhati on the first stage of her journey to England, and returning to Shillong, he had to be reminded by his butler that it was no use waiting for the memsahib to join him for dinner because she was no longer there. This DC filed his confidential papers in a cupboard which he kept carefully locked, but once he lost the key and called his orderly to force it open. "No need, Sahib", declared his more perceptive servant, pulling the cupboard away from the wall and revealing the fact that it had no back. It is not, perhaps, surprising that the bazaar telegraph was so efficient.

Pets were a frequent cause of dissension, as, for example, the shooting of a pet gibbon by an irate soldier who claimed it was endangering his children's lives, and which led to a civil action in the local court. There was also a rather mean woman who wished to mate her bitch with a well-bred dog owned by her friend, but demurred at the stud fee. She overcame this hurdle by taking her pet for walks past her friend's house until the desired union had been consummated. There was no court case on this occasion but it is on record that the two ladies, unlike their pets, ceased to be friends.

The Europeans of Shillong were very like other communities and, being also mortal, we sometimes required the services of a priest or doctor, but although eminent in the pulpit or the surgery, neither was always as sympathetic as might have been the case when dealing with the young. Indian hill stations were notorious for illicit love affairs, but Shillong had its fair share of innocents, who sometimes found marriage guidance hard to come by. One young man who asked the Government chaplain for marital advice was told that if he hadn't yet discovered the secrets of love he never would. Another potential bridegroom asked the civil surgeon for similar guidance. He was advised to lock himself in a room with his intended and find out for himself. Whether this practical but unusual advice was followed I don't know but both marriages appear to have been successful.

If one fell seriously ill or, having discovered the secrets of conjugal bliss, was about to give birth, there were two well-equipped hospitals, staffed by European doctors and Khasis. There was also the Pasteur Institute, where our three-year-old son received fourteen jabs in his small bottom after being bitten by a rabid dog. It was our lowly sweeper who heroically drove off and killed the mad animal with his broom. Such bites have to be treated promptly if the patient is not to contract rabies. It was fortunate for our son that the Institute was on our doorstep.

Most of the Khasis lived in neat and comfortable houses in a suburb of Shillong called Laitumkrah, and most were Christians. The majority of Khasi Christians are converts of either the Welsh Baptist mission or Roman Catholics, but there were other denominations. In the neighbouring Jaintia Hills district, a colleague of mine Pat Stracey, in his book *Reade Elephant Hunter* mentions eight separate denominations in the town of Jowai. This is not as many as the 250 recorded by a visitor to Cardiganshire at the beginning of this century, but is still quite a respectable number.

Some Khasi women had remarkable Christian names. One of my nurses in the mission hospital had a baby called 'Lenient Board' because, although it was illegitimate, she had not been given the sack by the hospital authorities.

Although the father is normally the head of the family, Khasi descent is reckoned on the mother's side. It is the girl who inherits the family possessions, and the woman takes the mate of her choice and plays the most active role. In pagan families illegitimate children are no problem — whoever the father, such a child becomes its mother's heir and one of the family.

Some Khasi girls have rosy cheeks and are usually attractive to male European eyes. Both sexes are extremely strong and carry heavy loads in baskets on their backs up the hills, usually by the shortest and steepest route. The babies, often carried by their not-so-big elder sisters, are swathed like mummies and strapped to the child's back so that its hands are free for other tasks. The great sport of the men is archery, which is accurately pursued with bows, arrows and strings made of bamboo.

The pagan Khasis, in common with the other hill tribes of Assam, worship, or at least attempt to propitiate, the spirits of the streams and hills, and their sacred groves of relict evergreen vegetation are a feature of many Khasi hill tops. One of these groves is on the Shillong Peak, named after U Shillong who discovered its spirit. The beautiful daughter of this spirit-god lived in the Marai cave but, although many would have liked to make love to her, the entrance to the cave was too narrow for lovers to enter. She was eventually lured out by a beautiful flower and married to her resourceful seducer, and 'The Flower of the Lured One' became the ancestress of the Siems of Khyrem and Mylliem.

The sacred groves are still carefully preserved, it being considered sacrilege to cut even a twig within them, except for ritual purposes, and the only building sanctioned in the vicinity of the Shillong Peak was the Governor's summer chalet. Unfortunately, the Khasi's respect for trees no longer extends beyond the precincts of the sacred groves. Elsewhere they are ruthlessly cleared for cultivation, to the detriment of the soil.

These sacred groves are of interest to botanists and ecologists because they are probably relics of the evergreen vegetation that is believed to have once clothed the hills. The evergreens were destroyed by the *jumiers* and replaced by more fire-resistant species of trees, bamboos and grass, covering a soil which grows excellent potatoes but is rapidly being eroded. The dominant tree is now the Khasi pine which used to be known as *Pinus Khasia* but, in the exasperating manner of botanists, is now called *Pinus Insularis* because it is also found in the aptly-named Philippines. The only other places where this species occurs naturally are the Naga Hills and Eastern Himalayas. The Nagas, who are thought to have cultural links with Indonesia and Melanesia, are seemingly also of the same mongoloid stock as the people of the Eastern Himalayas and the Khasis; and the Khasi pine, like these people, appears to have much the same distribution.

Another supernatural creature, in this case a monstrous snake called U Thlen, once lived in a cave at Cherrapunjee, where it terrorised the neighbourhood until one man, forced a red-hot piece of iron down its throat, and killed it. The snake's body was cut into small pieces but, unfortunately, one small piece was not, as instructed, eaten and from it sprang a host of little thlens. These unpleasant creatures attach themselves to people's property and will bring wealth and prosperity to the owners, but only if supplied with a diet of human blood. Otherwise, the family becomes poverty-stricken and destitute. A murder cult, to appease the thlens, sprang up as a natural corollary. Our children's ayah, although a Christian, was terrified of the thlens and nothing would have induced her to venture out alone at night.

Monoliths and flat stones, or dolmens, sometimes nearly thirty feet high, are another feature of the Khasi Hills. In some places there are nearly 30 monoliths in a group, usually in lines of three to five stones. One famous collection of these standing stones was erected to Kampat Wah, a woman who had divorced no fewer than thirty husbands, but whether this feat was the motive for the memorial is not clear. Another group consists of 300 stones and is said to have been set up by her grateful customers in memory of a woman who had run a popular eating house for travellers — presumably a 300 star hotel.

The monoliths are cenotaphs, and on no account may be moved, even if this means that the road has to be built round them. The actual graves are under special cairns and food is offered on the flat stones to the spirits of the departed, and particularly to the primeval 'grandmother' ancestress of the clan, ancestor-worship playing an important part in the lives of the pagan Khasis.

The Khasi woman normally wears a blue woollen cloak, below which protrudes the hem of her skirt covering her bare legs. Underneath the cloak she is swathed in several cocoon-like layers, which do nothing for her figure but are well-adapted for the often cold, damp climate of the hills. Next to her skin, the woman wears a blouse and petticoat and over these three strips of coloured silk, each knotted over the shoulder and, directly below the outer cloak, an inner one knotted round her neck. The Khasi man wears a shirt and dhoti, a loose turban and waistcoat, and also, perhaps, a coat and nowadays a pullover and, invariably, a scarf round his neck or wound round his head in place of a turban.

On festive occasions, both men and women are much more grandly attired in velvet jackets and dresses. The men also wear white cocks' feathers in their turbans, and the girls are sheathed in gold brocaded cloth. They wear gold or silver coronets on their heads, necklaces of wooden beads or coral, gold or silver, earrings and bracelets. The main occasion for dressing-up is the Nongkrem dance, originally performed in conjunction with the annual sacrifice to the ruling goddess of the State, when priests and priestesses offer up goats to ensure the prosperity of the clan. The great dance, with the girls shuffling round in the centre, and the men revolving around them in an endless circle, is the final ceremony. The celebrations continue all day, fresh dancers taking the place of those who have become exhausted, as they drop out.

It is, perhaps, understandable that dances such as this, intimately connected with pagan sacrificial rites, have been discouraged by the missionaries. There can be no regret for the passing of such pagan superstitions and fears, but it is a pity that this could not have been done without taking so much of the colour out of the converts' lives. The early Christian missionaries were, perhaps, wiser, transforming the Roman Saturnalia into Christmas and the pagan dieties into saints.

During and after the war there was less glamour about Shillong and things were quieter. I no longer looked on it as a holiday resort but as my place of work. Nevertheless, it retained much of its former charm. The ponies were a thing of the past and, instead of going for rides along Evelyn Ride, we took the children for picnics and gathered wild raspberries, or bathed in the rock pools. As senior conservator, I had inherited a 4-wheel drive, army-type station wagon which, I believe was known as a command car, and, during the cold weather of 1946–47, took my family as often as possible with me when I toured the plains. Time, we knew, was running out for us and, in fact, this proved to be our last cold weather in Assam.

We visited all our favourite haunts and a number of new ones — Christmas at Kulsi with red berries on the walls to simulate holly, the game reserves, the North Bank, where time seemed to stand still but was relentlessly speeding by, and the more intimate sal forests of Kamrup; the dense, sunless tropical rain forests of upper Assam. The deserted army camps and air strips, which for long had been ghost-like in their emptiness, were rapidly returning to jungle, with only the occasional incongruous notice or piece of rusty machinery still visible to remind us of the strenuous years of war.

Then the news broke that India was to be partitioned and that both India and Pakistan were to gain their independence. The Assam Government offered to keep me, but only on the strength of a contract which could be terminated by either party at the end of six months. I was full of malaria, had recently had a go of dysentary, and the children were rapidly reaching the age when they would need better schooling than they could get in India. Neither my wife nor I looked forward to separation. I decided, too, that with conditions so uncertain in India, it would be wiser to take the plunge and seek work at home while I was still young enough to find it. We decided to return home after the handover of power.

I was inundated with information about vacancies in the United Kingdom, but little of it had much attraction or appeared to match up to my qualifications. I appeared to be just too old to join the Forestry Commission and unqualified for most of the other available jobs, while that of milk recorder with the Milk Marketing Board had little appeal. I was, however, interested in farming. I had earned a proportion of my pension and, providing I was not employed by the British Government, was eligible for a reasonable sum of compensation for my loss of prospects in India. I decided to fulfil an old ambition and rent a small farm, but that is another story.

In the meantime, the summer drew on. Joy and I featured in a last group photograph on the lawn outside my Shillong office. On 15th August, 1947, Independence Day, my family and I gathered with those of other officials to see the Union Jack hauled down and the Indian flag hoisted in its place, while the band played the national anthems and the appropriate speeches were delivered. Then, feeling flat and unwanted, we returned home to tea.

The next few days were filled with packing and crating and the despatching of our heavier belongings to Calcutta, from where they would be shipped home. In next to no time the hour had come to say goodbye and leave Assam. We left behind our weeping servants, bundled our weeping children into the car and, near to tears ourselves, set off down the hill road which I had first climbed eighteen years before.

Partition, which had been forced on the British Government by the stubbornness of Jinnah, was reaping its first fruits, the massacre of several million Indians and Pakistanis, in the communal riots which followed the division of India. We had no idea what we should meet with on the journey to Bombay, but most of the trouble was, fortunately for us, confined to the North West, and we saw nothing of the bloodbath. Few Europeans, in fact, lost their lives, the purges being carried out by Muslims against Hindus and Hindus against Muslims. Practically the only Europeans involved were those Indian Army officers who, still attached to the Indian and Pakistani regiments, found themselves facing one another across the new borders. It was, nevertheless, a relief to be safely on board ship at Bombay, after a hot and humid wait in a tented transport camp.

The ship was crowded and the voyage uneventful until we reached Liverpool, except for my initiation into a game called Housey Housey, once known as Lotto, and which now, as Bingo, has become a national obsession. As the voyage came to its end, the passengers surged to the ship's side to get their first close-up of the home port. The ship, which carried no cargo and apparently no ballast, lurched dangerously to starboard, while the master frantically ordered the passengers back from the rails.

It was nice to be home and, after only a few months' absence we felt more at home than on our previous leave. All the same, it was like living in a vacuum — it is a change suddenly to find oneself out of a job after holding down a responsible position. It is a change too, to exchange a life in which one has had a wide circle of friends and acquaintances, for a life in which one's roots may be embedded but where one has become just number LFIZ05 5750 in the National Insurance register. England is a lovely country but, in 1947, it seemed to me too confining, too full and altogether too insular. It was, perhaps understandably, preoccupied with its own recent and present troubles, which we ourselves had not shared.

I was, in some ways, more homesick for India than I had ever been for my own country, and the 'homesickness' was to stay with me for a long time. There are, or were, some words engraved over the door of my Shillong office: 'You can take a man out of the forest, but you cannot take the forest out of the man', and that, I found, was only too true.